BEYOND THE FIVE SENSES

STORIES ON LIFE AND SPIRIT FROM INTERNATIONAL CLAIRVOYANT-MEDIUM, BERNICE ROBE-QUINN

LESLEY METCALFE

BALBOA.
PRESS
A DIVISION OF HAY HOUSE

Balboa Press books may be ordered through booksellers or by contacting:

Balboa Press
A Division of Hay House
1663 Liberty Drive
Bloomington, IN 47403
www.balboapress.com
1 (877) 407-4847

Because of the dynamic nature of the Internet, any web addresses or links contained in this book may have changed since publication and may no longer be valid. The views expressed in this work are solely those of the author and do not necessarily reflect the views of the publisher, and the publisher hereby disclaims any responsibility for them.

The author of this book does not dispense medical advice or prescribe the use of any technique as a form of treatment for physical, emotional, or medical problems without the advice of a physician, either directly or indirectly. The intent of the author is only to offer information of a general nature to help you in your quest for emotional and spiritual well-being. In the event you use any of the information in this book for yourself, which is your constitutional right, the author and the publisher assume no responsibility for your actions.

Any people depicted in stock imagery provided by Thinkstock are models, and such images are being used for illustrative purposes only.
Certain stock imagery © Thinkstock.

Printed in the United States of America.

ISBN: 978-1-4525-9562-7 (sc)
ISBN: 978-1-4525-9564-1 (hc)
ISBN: 978-1-4525-9563-4 (e)

Library of Congress Control Number: 2014906436

Balboa Press rev. date: 05/22/2014

For my brother
Anthony
1962 - 1968

"As a single footstep will not make a path on the earth,
so a single thought will not make a pathway in the mind.
To make a deep physical path, we walk again and again.
To make a deep mental path, we must think over and over
the kind of thoughts we wish to dominate our lives."

Henry David Thoreau

CONTENTS

FOREWORD

I have to say that it was with reluctance that I agreed to read a book claiming to explore what was beyond our five senses. As a consultant psychiatrist for more than twenty five years, people who claim to "hear", "see", or "feel" things that have no physical manifestation, have usually been patients. However, I was surprised to find a deeply spiritual dimension in this book that had something fresh to say about our "being". Not only was there a sincere humanitarian theme running throughout, I genuinely believe that this book could very much help people understand themselves better and make more sense of their lives.

Though the book is a very spiritual, there is no dogma or religious bias whatsoever. Many of the thought techniques relate to Cognitive Behavioral Therapy, or CBT, a universally accepted approach in the management of mild to moderate emotional disorders. I have personally used CBT for a large part of my career with considerable success.

Thoughts are truly phenomenal things. As Freud said, the human mind is like an iceberg with only 10% of the whole being evident as represented in conscious thought. The other 90%, though deeply buried in the unconscious mind, has a powerful role in shaping our thoughts, behaviors, and therefore our lives.

The way we allow ourselves to think is the building block of everything else. It is especially important to know how to strike a balance when life hits us with the unexpected. The power of thinking is crucial in situations like this.

Beyond the Five Senses is a book I would recommend to anyone seeking answers and meaning about the direction their life may be heading.

The power of the human mind is magnificent. This book goes some way to unravelling the monumental complexities and enabling personal empowerment.

Dr Emad Hussain
Fellow of the Royal College of Psychiatrists, London

INTRODUCTION

When I was a young child of five or six, I regularly had clairvoyant experiences and saw energies in and around objects and people. I was frequently told I had a "good imagination", even by my late first husband, as I was plagued with dreams which turned out to be premonitions about his death.

My involvement with this book began as nothing more than a casual favor. However, the more I got involved, the more I found myself drawn in.

It gradually became clear to me that the phenomenal powers I had been receptive to, especially in childhood, I had not only taken for granted, I had willfully chosen to push aside. I realised I had abandoned my innate intuition in favor of logic and that in some situations, this mind set was not only working against me, it was blocking me.

Through Bernice's stories on life and spirit, it became clear that all the powers of the universe were out there available for us to call upon and use to our advantage at any time. The main problem blocking most of us was our way of thinking.

From the backdrop of Bernice's thirty year career as a clairvoyant medium, this book presents a series of true, yet thought provoking stories, on life and spirit. Some of which will warm your heart; others will give you goose bumps. The desire to write this book came from a genuine desire to make a positive difference in the world. Throughout, there is humility and generosity of spirit that I have come to acknowledge as Bernice's trademark.

Lesley Metcalfe
Writer

PREFACE

Over the thirty or so years I have been working as a clairvoyant medium, I have seen and hopefully helped thousands of people to gain insight into their lives and the problems that may surround them. There is nothing I haven't seen, heard, or witnessed in my office and I can honestly say that I have encountered the best and worst of the human race over the years, to the point where I am no longer shocked by anything.

There are an infinite number of reasons why people come to see me, but the two most common ones concern relationship issues and bereavement. Sometimes a simple sentence can pull a person through a traumatic time in their lives and give them the hope and reassurance needed to carry them forward.

My own clairvoyant abilities began at the tender age of ten following a family tragedy. From this point onwards, I began to experience regular sightings of spirit around me at home. Whenever I looked in the mirror, I often saw spirit, especially my dead brother, looking back at me in the mirror. I was too young to question this, and just assumed everyone experienced such things. Not only did these experiences feed my curiosity to understand where this other place was, they also proved to me that there were other dimensions around, not only me, but *all* of us. How else would I be able to pick up on significant names, dates, places, etc. about people who are complete strangers? The point is that as these energies surround all of us, each and every one of us has the innate capacity, not only to connect with these dimensions, but to call upon them to use to our advantage.

One thing that so many clients have in common is that their way of thinking is the root of their problem, and they simply do not see the powers available to them through their thoughts.

The purpose of this book is to **show you how** to tap into this energy so that you can discover how to empower yourself and gain control over your life.

Beyond the Five Senses is a book that shares my journey through life and the things I have observed from my interactions with clients and spirit.

Acknowledgements

There are many people involved in the creation of any book. My thanks go to Lesley Metcalfe the writer, and to those who supported her work: Emad Hussain in particular, as well as Chris Sivewright, who both made invaluable contributions.

My gratitude also extends to my family and friends who have allowed me to be me. I am also eternally grateful to every client who has ever walked though my door and into my office. Each and every one of you has made an impact on me and taught me something very special.

May God bless you all.
This book is for *every one* of you, with love.

CHAPTER ONE

MY SECRET SPIRITUAL QUEST

"We still do not know one thousandth of one percent what nature has revealed to us."

Albert Einstein

Friday, May 8 1959

There was a very bad thunderstorm that morning, the worst in many years, or so I was told. That was the morning I was born. My mother often joked with me that my psychic abilities came through the ferocious electrical currents generated in that storm. What is most certainly true is that they didn't come through the teachings of the Catholic Church I was raised in. Like many religions, the Catholic Church has, by tradition, condemned psychics, mediums, and clairvoyants, - people like me - as heretics.

To put the record immediately straight, my faith in God is unshakeable. Over the many years I have been working as a clairvoyant-medium, I have met thousands of people and been able to pass on meaningful information concerning details and events surrounding their lives. This has proved to me time and time again that there are other dimensions beyond this

1

physical plane that have phenomenally powerful effects on our lives. Most of us are not consciously aware of the energies surrounding us, or their profound and continual effect on us. Instead, we go about our daily business, often stressed out and trying to get through the day.

It doesn't have to be this way.

It really doesn't because we all have the power to tap into these other dimensions and make them work with us to our advantage, thereby enriching the quality of our lives at every level. Gaining this knowledge ***will*** give you personal empowerment to live a happier, more successful life. That I can promise you!

My own starting point on this journey began at the age of ten following a family tragedy that changed my life completely and drove me inadvertently, to where I am now at every level of my adult life. I have had to work very hard on myself and my spirituality for many years to get to this level, not only as a clairvoyant, but also as a person.

The purpose of this book is to share that spiritual journey with you and the many experiences that accompany it, so that you too can discover how to tune into the same level of vibration, thereby empowering your own life at every level.

The Tragedy That Changed Everything

My childhood was rooted in a very loving, happy home and in many ways I had an idyllic childhood until my world was shattered by the tragic death of my younger brother, Anthony.

It was not long after my tenth birthday. Anthony was five years old and came home from school with sickness. The doctor diagnosed a gastric complaint, but my brother deteriorated very quickly and was later rushed into hospital with a strangulated hernia. Though surgeons operated,

Anthony contracted septicaemia shortly after the operation. Sadly, a few days later, he passed away. While Anthony was dying, he told my mother that he was floating on water and he was sailing away on a big ship.

Anthony was the seventh child in the family and my mother's first-born son. Being the only boy in the family at the time, he was doted on. My parents, especially my mother, never really got over his death but it was very painful for me too. I was very, very close to him.

> "It is during our darkest moments that we must
> focus to see the light."
>
> Aristotle Onassis

Onset of Clairvoyance

It was shortly after Anthony's death, that I started to "see" things. Lying in bed one evening, I saw the shadow of a person standing by my bedroom door, even though there was no one physically there to make the shadow. I saw this shadow several times, and then, sometime later, I saw a flash of light and then I could actually see a man and his shadow standing in the doorway. He was a solid figure, wearing a brown robe and appeared to be thumbing through the pages of a book. He glanced at me occasionally as he turned the pages. I accepted this as normal and didn't feel at all afraid of him. Thankfully, this is just as well because from this point on, I saw him on a regular basis in and around the family home. Several months later, my brother just "appeared", standing at the end of my bed, smiling. After this, I saw the man and my brother all the time and I never felt afraid.

> "Everyone who wills can hear the inner voice.
> It is within everyone."
>
> Mahatma Gandhi

When I first started having these visions, I was so excited. I wanted to tell everyone, "I've seen a man in my bedroom" or "I've seen Anthony standing at the end of my bed". I quickly realised it was best not to say anything. Whenever I tried, I was quickly rebuffed for making up stories. Of course, this was all said in complete innocence. It hadn't occurred to me as a ten year old that only I could "see" and that other people were not able to understand because they could not see anything themselves. I initially just assumed everyone could see things the way I could. In the end, I withdrew and didn't say anything.

Thirst for Knowledge

The regular sightings of my dead brother from the age of ten onwards filled me with happiness, but they also perplexed me deeply. If I could see him, then he must exist somewhere, but where was this place and why was I the only person who seemed to be able to connect to it?

As I progressed into adolescence, my visions of him no longer consoled me. In fact, they only fuelled my curiosity to discover where he might have gone and to try to contact him in the spiritual realm. However, there was a constant battle inside me. Even though I was driven to know more about this spiritual dimension, part of me believed that doing things you knew to be against the Catholic faith was sinful. Sure, I felt guilty. In fact, I felt guilty almost permanently but the need to contact Anthony was greater and gnawed at me, as did the search for answers to my questions about his whereabouts. I simply *had* to find out where he was. Though this quest began in my childhood, it continued into my adult life.

"So now faith, hope, and love abide, these three:
but the greatest of these is love."

Corinthians 13:13
(English Standard Version)

At the age of eighteen, I decided to seek out the advice of one of the world's most celebrated mediums, Doris Stokes. What an amazing lady she was! Miraculously, out of an audience of more than four hundred people, she picked me and said that there was a boy around me called Anthony. She also said that I was protected by spirit and would go on to do the same work she was doing. At the time, though I had regular sightings and experiences of other energies no-one else around me could sense, my ability to "see" was very much in its infancy and in spite of my secret spiritual quest, my beliefs were firmly rooted in the Catholic faith and my guilt trips compelled me to mass every Sunday.

Spiritual Quest for Truth

Since childhood, I knew there was a pure or divine energy source, but I knew very little about any other faith besides Catholicism.

One day, I stumbled on Norman Vincent Peale's book *The Power of Positive Thinking*. What was fresh and attractive in his approach was that this divine energy source was presented as *liberating positive source and force* that was loving and embracing for *everyone* who wanted to call upon that force, no matter what gender, religion or race. The message was loud and clear:

> "Change the way you think about God and you change your world. Change your thoughts and you change your world."
>
> Norman Vincent Peale

I read and re-read his books many times until I understood at progressively deeper levels. I also read extensively about world religions. It's interesting that the fundamental message or truth in all these major religions came down to pretty much the same simple message: love and kindness.

"There is no need for temples;
no need for complicated philosophies.
My brain and my heart are my temples;
my philosophy is kindness."

Dalai Lama

Divine Source Energy

I used to believe God was a man who lived up in the sky who looked down on each of us, aided by his army of helpers in the form of angels and saints. I believed these immortals spent all their time watching our every move, constantly making notes on a gigantic blackboard of our good and bad actions and thoughts. Of course, by the very essence of us being human, most of our "life list" would be a mixture of good and bad. At the end of our lives, God and his army of helpers were ready and waiting at the Pearly Gates with their long list of notes, ready to judge us and decide our fate with a ticket to heaven or hell. As God and his army lived on a moral high ground that no mortal could reach, most of us were doomed to receive a ticket to hell, not heaven.

This unforgiving, judgemental value system was how I viewed God when I was growing up. I now recognise how limiting and inhibiting this oversimplified view is. Nowadays it makes infinitely more sense to me that any divine power or energy source would have to be available to the whole human race, *as and when it is called upon*, no matter what gender, colour, or religion, and not be quite so harsh, judgmental, and unforgiving as I had been led to believe.

"Mankind is naught but a single nation"

Holy Qur'an

Over the years, my work has opened up another way of thinking and understanding entirely. I now recognise through experience that source energy or divine power isn't separated from us on some unreachable moral high ground, beyond human capability. Rather, it is part of us and we are part of it. What's more, its powers are available to us all to call on at any time. In other words, this energy is ready and waiting for all of us to tap into and use to our advantage. It is this knowledge I want to share with you.

Through the work I do, I have come to understand that we are all continually surrounded by energy, all of the time. Though many of these energies may be invisible to us, their effect on us is continuous. For example, gravity, magnetism, radioactivity, and so on. Though their effects vary, they are affecting us continually.

In a similar way, we are all constantly surrounded by non-physical source energy. If this energy wasn't surrounding each and every one of us, then I simply wouldn't be able to do my job. As we will explore, we do not need any psychic abilities to link with source energy. Whether we are consciously aware of it or not, and whether we like it or not, this energy is something each of us is constantly interacting with. How do we do this? We do this through our thoughts.

Once we understand the phenomenal powers available to us through this link, everything in our world is immediately empowered and liberated, and the possibilities for personal gain are infinite.

"Though we may know him by a thousand names,
he is one and the <u>same to us all</u>."

Mahatma Gandhi

Each and every one of us is like a mini radio transmitter, continually exchanging energy with the universe through our thoughts. Whether we are consciously aware of this or not, we constantly tune into the universe and it tunes into us through our thoughts. The process is automatic, involuntary and continual. We are all eternally linked into the universe through our own consciousness. Our thoughts are like an invisible thread, or umbilical cord, connecting us to the universe. Tremendous gifts are bestowed on us through this invisible connection, taking our abilities way **Beyond the Five Senses** we believe we are limited to. In other words, our thoughts are our sixth sense. Even though this sixth sense is a gift we all possess, for most of us, it is either underused or completely ignored. What a terrible waste of energy.

Instead of using our innate ability, we misguidedly believe that we are passive travellers on the journey of life, and that we have little or no control over our lives other than the mundane hum-drum essentials, like what we eat for breakfast or when we cross the road, and so on. Is it any wonder that our lives trundle along the same trajectory: day by day, week on week, year on year? We end up focusing on what is wrong, not what is right. Unless we make a conscious effort to change things, life just slips by seemingly out of our control. It is exactly this scenario that rings true for so many of the people who come to see me.

The good news is that by making subtle, yet deliberate changes in the way we think, we can use our gift or our innate sixth sense, or whatever you want to call it, to our own advantage. It is simply a question of the way we direct and channel our thoughts because, as we will explore throughout this book, every thought really does count.

If we want source energy to work with us to our advantage, then we have to make the effort to tune into it, not ignore it. Each of us has the innate ability to link or tune into this energy because it is part of us and we are part of it. Linking with divine source is very easy. All we have to do is make our thought energies harmonious with source, in other words, think happy, loving thoughts.

There is a direct link between the energy vibration of our thoughts and the energy we link with outside ourselves in the universe. So, by thinking positive, happy, all loving thoughts, we link with positive universal energy or divine source. Conversely, by thinking negative, resentful, unhappy thoughts, we link with negative universal energies.

In this way, our thoughts constantly link us with phenomenally powerful universal energies. By deliberately changing or managing the way we think, each of us has the power to attract phenomenal energies back to us.

> "All the powers of the universe are already ours.
> It is we who have put our hands before our
> eyes and cry that it is dark."
>
> Swami Vivekananda

As we will explore in the chapters that follow in this book, deliberately channelling or directing our thoughts requires minimal effort, yet the results are miraculous. This has been proved to me time and again. In fact, shortly after directing my way of thinking – literally a matter of weeks – I had one of the most amazing experiences of my life. Not only did it prove to me that the philosophy worked, it bowled me over and had me completely hooked and changed my life irrevocably.

Up until this point, I felt that my life had hit a brick wall. Still in my teens, I had nothing in the way of material things and was heading in an arbitrary direction. Armed with my new thinking strategy, I put out a thought requesting the right direction for my life path be revealed to me. I practised this thought over and over every day for two or three weeks. Rather like saying a prayer or a mantra, I repeated my request both silently to myself and out loud whenever I could, *focusing all my attention on it,* for example:

> "Please show me the way, I need direction,
> please show me the right path,
> please show me the way, I need direction,
> please show me the right path."

And so on, repeated over and over while focusing only on this request and blocking out all other "mind noise".

Days went by. Weeks went by. Nothing happened. It didn't matter. I was so desperately unhappy that I persisted, repeating the thought over and over, focusing my attention on the request so that my words and my thoughts sent out the same clear message or energy vibration of what I wanted and needed to come back to me. It is vitally important that thoughts and words echo the same clear message.

Quite out of the blue one evening, I woke up in my grotty bedsit in a moonlit room to find what I would describe as an extremely peaceful, serene atmosphere. As I lay in bed, my attention was taken to the corner of the room where I saw a huge ball of light flowing from one corner of the ceiling towards me. The light was an extraordinary vivid aqua-blue, and I just *knew* was full of life, love, and energy as it was spinning. I didn't feel endangered, quite the opposite in fact. As I watched, the light travelled slowly towards me, getting bigger and spinning faster. Somehow, it emitted overwhelming peace and power. It was so beautiful, and made me feel so serene that I couldn't help but reach out and touch it. In those moments, I felt so completely peaceful and filled with love. I suddenly sensed utter clarity about my purpose here on earth, and that my vocation was to help people. I simply knew and understood this.

I can only explain that in those moments I experienced a heightened state of perception and simply *knew* with complete clarity that this was the case. From this moment, I was hooked.

After this experience, I actively tried to open up my mind to other thought perspectives and read extensively on world religions and major spiritual philosophies, until I was able to understand at progressively deeper levels how shallow my own life was at the time.

"True wisdom comes to each of us when we realise
how little we understand about life, ourselves
and the world around us."

Socrates

Not only did my spirituality grow with this deeper understanding, I also noticed that my ability to communicate with spirit increased. Things just literally came to me without me even trying. I knew things about people without having any information, names, dates, places, and so on.

As I have already mentioned and as we will explore, there is no need to be clairvoyant to tune into this energy or reap the benefits it brings. We all have this sense and anyone who wants to open themselves up to it can benefit. By consciously directing our thoughts towards what we want or need help with, in as simple and clear way as possible, we can attract the divine energy closer to us and bring positive changes to our lives. Like everything else, the more we practise, the more skilled we become. Once we engage with the cycle, the loop is forever on-going.

There is nothing new in this philosophy. The fundamental ideas of this type of thinking can be found in many religions and spiritual teachings.

"Heaven means to be one with God."

Confucius

It is now thirty years since I first started out as a clairvoyant. In that time, I have helped thousands of people, not only through bereavement, but also through major life stresses, such as break-up of relationships and personal emotional turmoil.

Many people I have worked with fail to see that the way out of their problem is by redirecting their way of thinking. In fact, for some people their thinking habits may actually be working against them, not for them.

Thoughts determine behaviour and behaviour determines lives. Essentially, the way we think and the way we view ourselves in the universe is the most fundamental key to our existence because it is at the very core of everything else around us.

There is nothing special about me. I really believe and know this to be true. I know that I am just a channel that another energy or dimension passes through. It tunes into me because I tune into it and vice-versa and I am now an "easy target", if you like. Though the tragedy that kick-started my journey made me "open" from an early age, this really was only an initial catalyst on my journey. I have had to work very hard on myself and it hasn't always been an easy, painless journey. However, I thank God for opening my eyes to the knowledge that another world exists beyond this physical plane and that, whether we are aware of it or not, we are all always constantly in touch with that place through thought.

Channelling and directing our thinking may mean subtle changes, but the pay-offs are phenomenal in so many ways. In the very beginning, I really didn't understand the phenomenal power of the energy I was tuning into... I do now!!!

What is out there is truly magical yet so simple. It is this understanding that I want to share with you in the chapters that follow, so that you too can empower yourself and experience the joys of a happier, more fulfilling life.

CHAPTER TWO

HOW ENERGY WORKS

"Scientists were rated as great heretics by the church
but they were truly religious men because of their faith
in the orderliness of the universe."

Albert Einstein

In the last chapter, I touched on the power of thought as an energy, and how directing my way of thinking has given me empowerment over every area of my life. I am not only a happier, more fulfilled person, the overall effect on my life has been phenomenal.

Whether we are aware of it or not, our thoughts are the most powerful entity we possess as they are alive outside us and continually linking us with phenomenally powerful universal energies. However, for most of us, our thoughts remain largely untapped as a resource at our disposal.

To recap, we are all constantly surrounded by the abundant love and life force of the universe, or divine source energy. Each of us originates from this source, so it is part of us as we are part of it. Its powers are available to us all to call on at any time to use to our advantage. Every single one of us has the innate ability to tap into source energy by thinking thoughts that echo or match the same vibration as source. All we have to do is channel or direct our thinking so that our thoughts are abundantly positive in their essence: joyous, grateful, happy, vibrant, pure, etc.

"Where there is love there is God also."

Buddha

You Are What You Think

Though most humans believe they are limited to five senses, animals have maintained the need to use this instinctive sixth sense. Indeed, animals remain adept at reading energies. For example, it is a well-known fact that before an epileptic seizure, the balance of positive and negatively charged ions in the brain changes. What is interesting is that animals are able to detect this shift in energy. Our good old friend, the dog, can be trained to pick-up on these ionic changes, thereby forewarning the sufferer of a looming seizure before it happens.

Though animals may well be adept at reading invisible energies, the universe is masterly at it!

We may believe that our thoughts remain our private secret. Do not be fooled. Everything that we think and therefore feel, say or act out in behaviour, creates and sends out invisible energy waves or vibrations all of the time.

Telepathic Universe

The entire universe is filled with vibrating energies, positive and negative, the yin and yang or life balance. Even though we may not be consciously aware of it, our thoughts send out energy waves all of the time, and this in turn, links us with the same energy in the universe. Essentially, therefore, the universe is telepathic.

Unwittingly, our thoughts join us into an energy loop or thought-dialogue with the universe, so that whatever energy we send out through our thoughts is attracted back to us. In this way, our thoughts are literally alive.

We Create Our Own "Reality"

Each of us is constantly creating our own reality through our thoughts or consciousness. Over time, we become a product of our thoughts: our thoughts determine our behaviour, and therefore, our lives. It is how we choose to direct our consciousness that is the key.

"Watch your thoughts, they become your words.
Watch your words, they become your actions.
Watch your actions, they become your habits.
Watch your habits, they become your character.
Watch your character, it becomes your destiny."

Tao Tse

If we choose to think positive thoughts, we are tapping into the positive energies of the universe. Sending out such positive thoughts creates and brings back to us positive energy. In other words, by joining in the positive cycle through thought, we enter into a positive energy loop with the universe: we become part of it and it becomes part of us. Conversely, if we allow our consciousness to be preoccupied with problems, issues or regrets, then we are sending out negative thought vibes that link us with negative universal energies. Such thought processes draw us into a negative energy loop, and this brings more negative energy back to us.

For many years now, I have deliberately directed my thinking to tune into a positive energy loop. One way or another, I am constantly engaged within this thought-dialogue loop. It is precisely this connection that enables me to tune into the energies surrounding the clients who come to see me.

There is nothing clever or secretive in what I do. The fundamental principles I use to tune in my thoughts and provide information for clients come from exactly these same principles. The only thing that separates me from anyone else is years of practise: through practise we become skilled, and the more skill we attain the more automatic the skill becomes. In essence, this is the key.

How to Think Positive Thoughts

For those who may still be unsure, let us consider for a moment how to think a positive thought.

If we try for a few moments to look objectively at our own lives, examining all the good points as well as the less positive ones. No matter how hard our lives may seem, there *will* be positives. Focus on them.

For a start, each of us has a life and therefore, free will to *choose*. That's two positives already, there will be many others. Be objective. Write a list if it helps.

Having identified a few positives things, it is important to acknowledge them, one by one. For example, we each have a life, therefore free will. Acknowledge each positive and say thank you for it. Now move onto the next positive.

Engaging in the positive energy loop is really that simple. Focusing *only* on the positives in this way is the first step in changing our thinking. Notice how little effort it really requires to think a positive thought. Notice too how any low mood or feeling of powerlessness is diluted. Suddenly, our focus shifts to something we are in control of.

No matter what we believe, we really do have control over our thoughts, simply by making a conscious attempt to think in a slightly different way, even if only for a moment. This two-step process of recognising the positives and saying thank you for them is the starting point of the magic.

Though it may seem grossly oversimplified it is incredibly effective. The longer we spend focusing and saying thank you for what we like and appreciate in our lives, the more empowerment we give ourselves. The magic is that the more we tap into this way of thinking, the more positive energy we get back. With practise, things are attracted towards us, and the more we practise, the more things are drawn to us, until the benefits of this way of thinking become abundantly obvious.

I have been practising this philosophy for so long that my communication through positive thoughts is automatic. The reason I am receptive to the energies surrounding my clients is because I am continually engaged in this energy loop.

"A man is the product of his thoughts:
what he thinks he becomes."

Mahatma Gandhi

Thinking in this way has enabled my ability as a clairvoyant medium to grow and develop. It has also brought a multitude of benefits and insights. I will share these with you in the chapters that follow. For now, I want to emphasise the simple point that thoughts are phenomenally powerful things. This power is available to all of us, free of charge and is life changing. It's such a terrible waste that most of us ignore this innate gift.

Thoughts Are Living Things

By directing our thoughts in the right ways, we can attract powerful energies back to us to work to our advantage.

Over the years, I am now in continual thought dialogue: I feed into it, it feeds back to me. When I talk to the universe through thoughts, I ask for help on big matters as well as very small matters, even something as seemingly mundane as a car parking space. What is interesting is that I *always* get a parking space… and, I always say thank you.

"When the solution is simple, God is answering."

Albert Einstein.

No matter how "coincidental" it may seem for the thing you have asked for to materialise, you *must* always say thank you. Acknowledgement is a way of sending back the love you receive. The more love and positivity you send back, the more you will get back, and the more you receive and appreciate, the more will come back to you.

This is the way the universe works. Trust me. It really is true and it really is liberating!

The way we live our lives and the extent we allow our free will to grow towards the positive, or divine, is a decision we make for ourselves. We all have the free will to make choice. We may choose to carry on with our habitual focus on the things that are wrong in our lives. In this case, we lock ourselves into exactly the same energy loop, so that the things that keep on going wrong for us, just keep on going wrong for us.

Alternatively, we can choose to make our predominant thought habits optimistic ones that focus on the things that are good, vibrant, and positive. Though this requires conscious effort, it draws us into an energy loop that brings enormous rewards into our lives.

Every Thought Counts

Every thought really does count, and it is important to guard our thoughts at all times. As we have touched on, positive thoughts bring positive energy back to us, and negative thoughts (the default for most people) bring back more negative things. It really is as simple as that.

I deliberately try to avoid thinking negative thoughts because they block positive energy coming towards me. If ever anyone upsets me or treats me badly, I always try to pray for them. Using strategies like this, I avoid tapping into any negative thoughts where I may feel bitter or harbour resentment.

"All that we are is the result of what we have thought.
If a man speaks or acts with an evil thought, pain follows him.
If a man speaks or acts with a pure thought,
happiness follows him like a shadow that never leaves him"

Buddha

Keep the Balance

No one is perfect. It is a normal human reaction to get irritated or annoyed with someone who upsets us. My point is that it is important to keep the balance tipped in favour of the positive energy vibes.

Whenever things feel gloomy, or we feel like we're thinking more negative thoughts than positive ones, either about others or ourselves, it is important to manage and divert the negative thoughts so they do not spiral and dominate our way of thinking. If ever this starts to happen, push out the negative thought by thinking a positive one to cancel it out. There are always ways of blocking or diverting negative thought energies, the key point is to be aware that we are thinking in a negative way. This is especially important when our thoughts drift back to past events that make us feel insecure or inadequate or angry, etc. These negative feelings overshadow any chance of happiness in the present as they continually colour our here and now. This not only affects our mood in the moment, it plays on our self-confidence and self-belief in detrimental ways.

"God has given us one tremendous instrument of protection
more powerful than machine guns, electricity,
poisonous gas, or any medicine - the mind."

Paramahansa Yogananda

We have all experienced injustice at some point or another, and we all have regrets. This is part of life. It is vital to remember that what is past is literally in the past and beyond our control. What cannot be changed needs to be let go of.

Never revisit the past with regret and sorrow for what could have been. These are negative thoughts that only pull us down and prevent us moving forward. We must never allow ourselves to dwell in a negative thought space for prolonged periods of time.

Another way to divert and manage negative thinking is to be conscious of how we think and *feel* in the immediate moment. Since we cannot change the past and we cannot engineer the future until it happens, the only control we have is in the present moment.

Sadly, unhappiness and dissatisfaction are the most common states of mind in our "civilised" Western culture. We spend too much time worrying, festering, and resenting. This is all wasteful and negative. So many of the clients who come to see me do so because their thoughts and behaviours are focused on a problem, for example, through worry, fear, jealousy, bitterness, greed, and so on. Sometimes, such thoughts are directed towards willing harm to others, or worse, following through these thoughts with destructive actions.

"There is nothing that wastes the body like worry,
and one who has faith in God should be ashamed
to worry about anything whatsoever."

Mahatma Gandhi

Negativity, as I will look at in the next chapter, is very dangerous and damaging and only breeds more negativity, such as illness and misery.

Suffering Has the Power to Enrich Us

Even though some people may seem to sail through life unscathed by problems, nobody has a completely trouble-free life. All of us experience life's "banana skin" moments at some point. Whenever problems arise in our lives, it is important to accept and understand that any upset or crisis that hurts us emotionally opens up our spiritual development.

It is how we overcome life's struggles that gives our soul wealth and depth. Even in the worst of times, it is vital to never ever give up on positive thinking. Even in adversity, there is positivity.

"Adversity and suffering introduces a man to himself"

Unknown

It is natural to feel low, vulnerable or even desperate when we are faced with big problems. This applies to all of us, no matter how adept we become at managing our thinking, or how unshakeable our faith. No one has a completely trouble free life, but it is important to remember that during any time of major change, upset or crisis, we can learn great things and make ourselves wiser, greater people.

In times of real suffering, it is vitally important to accept things and not rage against them. Rage and anger only make matters worse. I know from personal experience that emotional pain and loss hurts. I have lost four babies, a set of twins through miscarriage and two life threatening ectopic pregnancies. Instead of thinking, *"Why me?"* now I try to think, *"Why should it not be me, what is so special about me above all others?"*

Such life experiences touch our souls deeply. Any trouble or difficulty is a lesson for our spiritual progression. It is how we face and deal with problems and overcome them that gives us great knowledge, empathy, and wisdom. Even though it may not seem so at the time, life's lessons are always spiritually enriching. The wisdom we gain brings us closer to divine source, and therefore brings a richer harvest back to us.

"Life is 10% what happens to you and 90% how you respond to it."

Unknown

Remember, whenever you have a bad experience, there will be a tremendous lesson in that experience somewhere: always look for ways to turn the negative into a positive. Negative thought patterns must be avoided at all costs.

CHAPTER THREE

NEGATIVE THOUGHTS NEED HEALTH WARNINGS!

"There is no limit to the power of the human mind.
The more concentrated it is, the more power is
brought to bear on one point; that is the secret."

Swami Vivekananda

We all have the free will to control our thoughts. Directing and channelling our thoughts for our own empowerment requires very little effort and is incredibly simple: identify the positives in our life and acknowledge them with gratitude.

This is the starting point of tuning in. Whenever we make a conscious, deliberate attempt to focus, we are sending out very strong energies. The universe is not only listening in, it is also responding to these thoughts by sending back the same energy vibes we have sent out. The effect of this tuning in process has a phenomenal impact on us.

As we explored in the last chapter, whether we are consciously aware of it or not, *we attract back our dominant thoughts.*

By being constantly focused on issues and problems, we allow negative thoughts to dominate our minds, thereby inviting more of the same back towards us. In this way, we slowly lose control over life and dig ourselves into a rut.

Focusing on what is wrong rather than what is right is exactly the mindset that so many people come to see me with: they feel trapped in a cycle that they feel powerless to get out of. What they simply cannot see, is that often they themselves are the creators of their own problem, and that their way of thinking is working against them not for them.

If we really want our lives to change and stop being the victim of circumstance, it is vitally important that we really take the message on board. Thoughts are alive like powerful magnets in the universe and draw back to us the same energy we send out. If our thinking is dominated by negative thought patterns, we invite more negative vibes back towards us. We therefore also inhibit and block positive energy coming towards us and we cannot access the magical source energy.

"It is our own mental attitude which makes
the world what it is for us.
Our thoughts make things beautiful,
our thoughts make things ugly.
The whole world is in our own minds.
Learn to see things in the proper light."

Swami Vivekananda

Negative Thought Patterns are Damaging

Negative thought patterns really do need health warnings. Not only do they make us feel down and miserable, they trap us in a negative loop that prevents us from tapping into the magic outside ourselves.

Life is never a completely trouble-free smooth journey for any of us. No one has a perfect life, and things happen that are completely beyond our control. It simply isn't possible to be positive all of the time. It is essential, however, to accept and recognise that life is not controlling us: we are the controller of our own life and the starting point of this control comes from how and what we allow ourselves to think.

Sometimes, it is very easy to allow negativity to creep up on us in our daily lives without even noticing we are losing our faith in the positive, or that our dominant thought patterns are shifting from positive to negative. It happens to us all and is part of life. This is why it is important to make a conscious effort to manage our thoughts.

Rather like showering and cleaning your teeth, it is vital to set aside a time when you *make* yourself think positive thoughts. I start as soon as I wake up in the morning and continue while I am showering, and getting dressed, etc.

Once we start to practise this way of thinking, it quickly becomes automatic and positive changes start to draw towards us. This reinforces our faith in the process, and faith breeds more faith, and so on. Training ourselves to *think* in a very slightly different way brings about hugely positive transformations to our lives.

The biggest obstacle blocking our access to this empowerment comes from our own negative thoughts. Negative thought patterns really do affect our lives in detrimental ways. Teaching ourselves to manage our thoughts not only helps us to block negative thoughts and feelings, it also has enormous benefits on our self-esteem.

Negative thought patterns restrain us; positive thought patterns liberate us.

"There is nothing noble in being superior to some other man.
The true nobility is in being superior to your previous self."

Hindu proverb

The purpose of this chapter is to explore how easily negative thought patterns can establish within us, far more easily than positive thought patterns it would seem! The key danger zone of negative thinking comes from our own thought habits. Often, we are our own worst enemy in this matter as our thought habits are the very thing restraining us.

Often, however, our negative thoughts originate from the seeds of doubt sown into us by another person's words or behaviours. Being aware of the sources of negative thought, inside and outside ourselves is, I believe, half the battle when it comes to thought management and staying focused in the positive domain.

Negative Thinking from Our Own Thoughts

Most people engage in negative energies without even knowing that this is what they're doing. That in a nut shell is the problem: they are not consciously aware that they are continually thinking in this way or of the damage they are doing to themselves in the process. All of us have stresses, worries, and anxieties.

It is how we manage them that is crucial.

Anxiety and worry are enormous negative energies that will, if we allow them to, disintegrate and destroy our happiness and eventually dominate our life. Worry, fear, and insecurity are modern thought diseases.

> "And which of you by worrying can
> add a single hour to this life's span?"
>
> Luke 12:25
> (New American Standard Bible)

As we have established, by allowing ourselves to worry, or feel insecure, etc., we are unwittingly inviting the same energy back to us. We become a worrier by adopting the worry philosophy. Quite simply, the more we worry, the more anxious and worried we become. The worry cycle is very self-perpetuating unless we make a conscious effort to stop it.

Apart from worry and anxiety, another common negative thought pattern is self-pity. Self-pity is incredibly self-destructive. In dwelling on the "Poor me... Why me?" thought vibe, we allow ourselves to become a victim of our own life and believe we are not in control, thus enabling more negative thought patterns to fester and grow.

Sometimes, people come to me with problems and really believe that they are the only person to have ever had that bad experience. Self-pity is a dead-end street that only leads to bitterness and resentment. We must never allow ourselves to delve into self-pity and believe that we are the only person to ever suffer. There is always someone worse off.

"Drop the idea that you are Atlas carrying
the world on your shoulders.
The world will go on without you.
Don't take yourself so seriously."

Norman Vincent Peale

We can all feel down and get stressed or do silly things that we may regret. We are all human and so we all make mistakes. The problem is that when we allow ourselves to dwell more in the negative zone than the positive, we are in danger of doing ourselves serious harm.

Preoccupations with jealousy, bitterness, money, and materialism, etc. are negative thoughts. By dwelling on them, we not only make ourselves feel miserable and powerless by our perceived state of inertia, we also repel positivity coming towards us, making our low mood lower. In this way, negative thought patterns dramatically reduce our opportunity to engage with positivity at any level. Negative thoughts and feelings should be avoided at all costs because they trap us in a bad place.

It really doesn't matter whether the negative thoughts are directed outwardly towards others as nastiness, envy, and so on, or whether they are directed inside ourselves as worry and insecurity, the effect on us is the same. Clearly, it may be a different story for the others who receive our nastiness, but that's another story! Negativity blocks positivity and locks us into bad thought loops. Ultimately, not only are we making ourselves and everyone else miserable, we are also making ourselves susceptible to negative attack.

Low depressed thoughts attract more low depressed thoughts. Entering this negative loop only serves to make our low thoughts even lower, and so the negative loop grows.

I cannot stress enough the dangers of negative thought energies. Negativity loves more negativity, especially when it comes to the worry monger: worry makes more worry. This can so easily mushroom. What may begin in a person as anxiety can easily turn into a serious depression.

> "When a man has an exact knowledge about
> the nature of thoughts he recognises those
> which are about to enter and defile him."
>
> Isaiah the Solitary

Remember, our thoughts create the world we live in, so if we feel any hint of a negative thought, such as jealousy, resentment, stress, and so on, always try to push out the negative thought with a positive one so that our thoughts raise above that level. This same thought management process is currently widely used in psychological medicine as therapy for conditions such as depression and anxiety, a treatment known as

Cognitive Behavioural Therapy or CBT: identify the negative thought and attack it with a positive one.

Remember, negativity can only get to you when you let it. Never forget that you are in control.

Negative Thinking from the Words of Others

Negative thoughts come from negative ideas. For many of the people I see, the seeds of negative ideas come, most of the time, from what other people have either said or done to them.

Negative ideas can be extremely damaging when they are planted into our thoughts. I would like to explore this with you so you can be aware how other people's energies feed into and off our own energies through behaviour and words.

The Power of Words

In the line of work I do, there are many charlatans who claim to be working with spirit. Sometimes, mediums pick up a person's worries and fears through telepathy and present these as messages from spirit. Their messages may well come from spirit, but be aware that they may well be working on a *negative* level. These people can be very dangerous and damaging if we listen to their advice and consider it to be truthful, positive information. Often what they say can be frightening, threatening and upsetting. The effect is that we go away worried, thereby enabling negativity to invade our thought space, starting with anxiety.

Just as a positive comment can boost someone's confidence to believe that all will be well, negative comments can really batter and hurt someone's soul. This is a painful thing I learned first-hand long before I even contemplated working as a clairvoyant.

"Guard your mind and you will not be harassed by temptations.
But if you fail to guard it, accept patiently whatever trial comes."

St Mark, the Ascetic

Guard Your Mind – Be Careful Who You Listen to!

In my late teens, I visited a clairvoyant who seemed to be a very nice, charming lady and gave me all sorts of information that seemed to be relevant to my life. Then all at once during the reading, she said *"You can take bad news, can't you?"* Being a polite naïve teenager, I said *"Yes, of course I can"*, not really thinking about the implications of what I was saying.

She went on to tell me that my mother was dying and that this was going to happen very soon. Though my mother had rheumatoid arthritis and had been ill for some time, she was not in any state to be considered at death's door. The shock of what the medium told me upset me hugely.

At this stage in my life, my own psychic abilities were very much in their infancy. Though I often saw Anthony and other spirits looking back at me when I looked into a mirror, my ability to link beyond this level was never really tested, mainly because I didn't understand what was being shown to me and therefore, didn't know how to do develop it. I believed back then that all clairvoyants were automatically wholesome spiritual people and spoke only in good faith. I didn't have the skills to question whether her prediction was correct or not, and therefore believed what she had said must be correct.

Driving home was a long hazy journey as I couldn't concentrate. My thoughts were entirely negative and I was preoccupied with worry about how I would break the bad news to my family, but I was even more distressed about how we would all cope with her loss as some of my brothers and sisters were still very young. I was simply devastated and as I drove along, I became so upset I had to stop the car and just sob.

As I pondered doom and gloom, I noticed that across the road from where I parked was a Spiritualist church. Equally, quite by chance, people were going inside the church for a service right at that very moment. At that time, I believed that going into a Spiritualist church was sinful and so dismissed the idea of joining the congregation. Whatever rationale came over me, I have no idea, but I decided that my need was greater than my guilt and that I would go inside the church anyway. I sneaked inside and sat as inconspicuously as possible at the back, listening intently to the sermon. I was eighteen.

The visiting clairvoyant began to speak, giving messages to people from spirit. Suddenly, he pointed straight at me and bellowed in a Yorkshire accent,

"There's no graves being dug here girl, so get that rubbish out of your head!"

I left the church feeling that a great weight had been lifted off my shoulders and drove home completely at peace.

Thankfully, the Yorkshire man with the bellowing voice who initially made me shoot out of my seat had been able to pick up on my thoughts and put my worried mind at rest.

"Gentleness, self-sacrifice and generosity are the exclusive possessions of no one race or religion."

Gandhi

Also thankfully, the clairvoyant's prediction was totally wrong, and my mother did not pass away until fourteen years later. Just imagine the damage I could have caused had I listened to her advice and broken the bad news! Had the seed of that thought entered my mother's belief system, I firmly believe it could have created extreme anxiety for her and even lead to a premature death.

I will never know why the clairvoyant told me this dreadful news or what her motives could possibly have been but it taught me two very valuable lessons: one, words are powerful, and two, be very careful who you listen to. This doesn't just apply to clairvoyant readings, but everyday conversations. What is said cannot be unsaid or taken back. Insensitive wording can create tremendous upset and anxiety, especially if such information is presented as "fact" from spirit.

I strongly believe that it is not right to pass on bad news of disaster or death to anyone. If you ever consult a clairvoyant who likes the drama of hard-hitting, negative news, I would advise you to be extremely sceptical of anything they say. Their warning, no matter how real or made up, is extremely dangerous and can have potentially disastrous consequences for the client who believes this information to be the truth. To forewarn someone of an impending death or disaster they are powerless to act over is completely immoral.

Clairvoyants who impart such negativity have no idea of the magnitude of energies they are working with. If you ever come across someone who claims to be working with spirit who is imparting news of death or disaster, I strongly advise you to physically remove yourself from their space.

Whenever I see a problem arising for a client, I always try to focus on the positive aspects surrounding them, so that they feel empowered to cope with anything that comes their way with confidence and self-belief, not extreme anxiety.

The Effect of One Sentence

Words have profound meanings. I have noticed time and again with my clients that a simple sentence or two can have a dramatic impact on the way a problem is perceived. Sometimes, a few words may become the thread of hope that pulls a person through a traumatic time. This point is most easily demonstrated in the example that follows.

When I first started doing clairvoyant readings thirty years ago, we had no central heating in the house, and my office was heated by a two-barred electric fire that I always kept on for clients when it was cold. The only gas appliance was the cooker in the kitchen.

One day, a young lady came to see me who I had never met before. As soon as she entered my office and sat down, I had an instantaneous sensation in my nose of the smell of gas. It was literally as though someone had squirted gas up my nostrils. It was such a strong sensation that it literally made me gag. She looked very perplexed and startled. Conscious that she may be worried herself, I turned off the electric fire and apologised to her about the overpowering smell of gas, explaining that the gas leak must be coming from the cooker in the kitchen.

Her eyes widened and her jaw dropped slightly. For several seconds she just stared at me silently. Then, with the same blank expression, she explained that I had already provided her with the proof she needed, and said that her husband had committed suicide by gassing himself in the oven.

As soon as she told me this, the pungent smell filling my nostrils evaporated completely.

Though I went on to give her late husband's name and some of the issues around him at the time he took his own life, what I said to her about the smell of gas completely changed her perception of what had happened. It proved to her that her husband was around her and justified her visit to see me.

Just a few words completely changed the way she thought about this terribly traumatic situation. One sentence gave her tremendous reassurance and empowered her to move on with her life.

"Everything on earth has its birth place in factory of the mind."

Paramahansa Yogananda

The way we think about something, is the key to everything else.

This brings me to another vitally important point that I believe this story demonstrates very clearly and simply, and that is, all the energy that I was able to tap into and pick up on was all around this young woman. It wasn't me who created it; it was already there, even though this client was completely unaware of it. It doesn't matter whether we are aware of these energies or not, they exist all around us and are constantly affecting us. The only difference between me and the client in this instance was that I was able to link into this dimension. I did this through the power of thought and the information was given to me.

I want to really emphasise here that the energies that surround us are not only there, they are also phenomenally powerful. How else would I be able to tap into them? If I can tap into the other dimensions surrounding people, then they don't only exist around me, and must exist all around each and every one of us. By allowing ourselves to be sucked into a negative energy loop, we block positive energy and entrap ourselves in a bad space. For me to relay relevant information to clients, who are often complete strangers, I am tapping into exactly the same energy loop that everyone else unwittingly taps into through their thoughts and consciousness. The only difference is that I am more sensitive to tuning in because I have spent years making a conscious effort to do so through practise. I do not profess to know what all these energy dimensions are, or that I have any greater skill than anyone else in picking them up.

I have, through practise, made a deliberate routine of tuning into this energy loop by managing the vibration of my thoughts to ensure they are positive ones.

This thought energy is the same for all of us. Whether we are daydreaming or deliberately and consciously trying to tap into it, as I do, the effect is the same. Deliberately or inadvertently, we are all tapping into the same energy source.

"Where can we go to find God if we cannot see Him
in our own hearts and in every living being."

Swami Vivekananda

The Magic Outside Ourselves

Thoughts enable us to tap into the phenomenally powerful energies that surround us all. This is demonstrated in the following example and concerns a couple who came to see me for the first time, so I knew nothing about them.

When they arrived they looked quite uptight and nervous. As soon as they sat down opposite to me, I immediately sensed that I was being pinned to the wall by my throat. Straight away, I asked them if they knew anyone who had hurt their neck recently. They said that they did know someone. After they said this, the grip around my neck became tighter and more intense and I had an overwhelming feeling that I was being strangled, so I went on to say just that.

The couple were silent for a few seconds and then told me that their daughter had been strangled by her husband who was now in prison for her murder.

As soon as they told me this, the pressure around my neck immediately eased and, thankfully, I felt released from the grip.

I was able to give their daughter's name, and the area of the house she was strangled in. I also felt strongly that there was another person involved in the murder as well as the convicted husband. This was confirmed to be the case when I was able to pick up on the names of the husband and the accomplice.

This poor bereaved couple had arrived at my office looking like walking zombies. The information I managed to pass onto them about their murdered daughter, for example, names, circumstances of death, etc., gave the bereaved couple the positive reassurance they needed to grieve and start to heal. They were shocked but *knew* the energies around them that I picked up were real.

These moments are very bitter sweet. It is distressing for the bereaved to be reminded of their loss, but so rewarding to know that their loved one is around them. Communicating this kind of information is very rewarding for me. It shows how just by imparting a few meaningful words to someone can have a dramatic effect on a person's way of thinking and consequently, everything else around them. When things feel less daunting and hopeless, healing can begin. This is in no way meant to underestimate the pain of bereavement, which I know from personal experience to be horrendous.

"No one ever told me that grief felt so like fear."

C.S. Lewis

Time for Change

I talk a lot about spiritual matters with my clients and I see a lot of young people who have absolutely no beliefs in any higher power, let alone any conventional religious beliefs. Yet, when I am able to link with a family member who has passed over, a grandmother, for example, many people "blindly" accept the information without questioning its source or origins. When I ask the client how they think I could get this information if there is *no* other dimension whatsoever, they have no answer. It's as though I am the first person to ever ask them anything spiritual. Hopefully, they leave my office and start to think about what I am saying and question life at a deeper level for themselves.

It really is time to change this blissful ignorance and accept that there really are phenomenally powerful forces operating beyond our limited five senses and that the biggest obstacle blocking most of us from accessing this magic is our own negative thought patterns. As we have explored in this chapter, negative thought patterns can be caused by the way we allow ourselves think. They can also come from the words of others who may plant seeds of doubt inside us. If we want our lives to work for us rather than being a victim to circumstance, it is vital to manage negative thoughts from inside and outside ourselves. By managing our thinking, each of us can tap into the magic of abundance.

CHAPTER FOUR

POSITIVE ENERGY HIJACKERS

"A person will worship something, have no doubt about that.
We may think that our tribute is paid in secret in the dark
recesses of our hearts, but it will out.
That which dominates our imaginations and our thoughts
will determine our lives, and our character.
Therefore, it behoves us to be careful what we worship,
for what we are worshipping, we are becoming."

Ralph Waldo Emerson

We have established that our thoughts are living energies in the universe, linking us into phenomenally powerful energies *Beyond the Five Senses* we believe we are limited to. This linking-in process happens whether we are consciously aware of it or not, and brings back to us the same energy we send out through our thoughts. Positive brings more positive and conversely, negative brings more negative. Positive thoughts liberate us, and negative thoughts restrain us. Managing the way we think is the greatest empowerment we can give ourselves. In the last chapter, we explored how our own negative thought patterns can block and trap us. Apart from our own thinking habits, negativity can also come from external influences.

It is my firm belief that the biggest obstacle most people face in trying to gain control over their lives is that they are unable to identify what negativity is in the first place. If we don't know what to look out for, we cannot avoid or stop its influence. Negativity is an extremely insidious energy, and can literally creep up on us so slowly that we don't really notice it happening. This is especially true for nice people who do not think in bad ways, so it is even harder for them to identify those external factors around them that are problematic or negative. Negativity is very real and very dangerous, so it is vital that we are able to recognise it so we can protect ourselves. I want to explore this with you here.

For most of us, a common general feeling of negative energy is feeling down or in a "flatter", more depressed mood than normal. This happens to us all from time to time. We all have bad times when we feel the need to offload onto a friend or family member. By talking about something that has upset us, we can share our problem with someone else, and thereby start to shed the negative vibes and begin to heal.

Drains and Radiators

Friends and family who uplift and support us are our *Radiators*. When we spend time around a Radiator, we experience the "feel-good" or "buzz" factor, as we pick up on their good energy vibes. This energy rubs off on us and we leave them feeling vibrant and happy. Radiators are givers of energy.

However, there are some people, and we have all met them, who no matter what, do not want to let go of their problem. Rather, they choose to focus on themselves and their problem so that they can be the centre of attention and gain our sympathy. These people are *Drains* as they drain the energies of others, and make us feel tired, zapped and deflated.

Although it is impossible to always be a *Radiator* and never a *Drain*, we are all a complex mixture of both, it is important to be aware of people around us who *perpetually* make us feel drained, empty and exhausted.

Drains can zap our energies in many ways, but one of the most common is through their topic and tone of conversation. I call these "Yes, but…" conversations. In other words, whatever problem they raise, any suggested solution will be greeted by "Yes, but…" whereupon they proceed to give reasons as to how they have tried that solution, why it failed, and why they are still the victim of circumstance who must be pitied at all costs.

"He who learns but does not think is lost!
He who thinks but does not learn is in great danger."

Confucius

Perpetual Drains Become Psychic Vampires

Perpetual Drains eventually become what I call Psychic Vampires, because they literally drain the life force out of us. That is really not good to be around!

These people are extremely negative and need the energy of others' to indulge in. It isn't possible to have healthy relationships with Perpetual Drains for prolonged periods of time as their negative energies start to rub off on us.

It is not acceptable for any healthy person to perpetually feed off another person's energy. We must all be aware of people who zap our energy and try not to become overly involved. We all have the free will to choose who and what we link with and we shouldn't feel guilty about moving away from difficult people.

Our thoughts and behaviours are our own responsibility and no one else's. We are all here to learn and cannot learn another person's lessons for them. There is a cut off between helping someone who is in genuine need because we are a nice person and allowing ourselves to be used as the feeding mechanism of another person's negative energy. Not only will Psychic Vampires use our energies and drain us, they will also block positivity coming towards us and this brings us further down.

It is especially hard for nice people to see through the motivations of the Perpetual Drains or Psychic Vampires.

Be aware! Some nasty people are dangerous and see our "niceness" as weakness. They do not care about others' or their feelings, they only care about themselves and so will use kindness limitlessly. Nasty people like this are not our friends. Some nasty people will even consciously try to do you harm just to inflate their own ego.

"An insincere friend is more to be feared than a wild beast;
a wild beast may wound your body,
but an evil friend will wound your mind."

Buddha

Whoever we bring into our life, we are going to be influenced by their thoughts and behaviours. So, it is essential to be careful who we link with and who we allow into our life.

When we surround ourselves with negative people, we will start to think like them and very quickly, they lower the level of our thinking, thus making their negative impact even harder to spot.

Stay away from negative people who perpetually bring us down - they are not our personal responsibility.

Usually, when people come to see me, especially for the first time, they come for a specific reason to gain insight into a particular issue or problem. For so many of the clients I see, it is often the relationships around them that are the main source of their problem. These relationship problems can be anything from affairs of the heart, to general family matters, to working relationships. The list is endless! However, relationship issues are by no means always the whole story. Negativity can come from many external influences beside people. For example, it is becoming an increasing problem that one of the biggest sources of external negativity I see is due to over indulgence in alcohol.

---

*"The evil of the world is made possible by
nothing but the sanction you give it"*

Ayn Rand

Alcohol Use and Abuse

When our own energies become imbalanced, our emotional resolve gradually drains away and we can become "fed up". This is a common feeling and for so many people the solution is to have a glass of wine – or two! This is fine every now and again. The problem arises when it becomes a crutch and we slide into alcohol-dependency. As time goes on, we unwittingly draw back to ourselves more and more negativity.

For example, I have read for many Prison Officers over the years. Though I truly admire these people, one thing most of them have in common is that they drink too much alcohol. There is a very negative side associated with their occupation: they spend all day with negative people who have done bad things and often find themselves under threat at work. A client of mine has had his life threatened several times. Obviously, alcohol indulgence helps to combat the feeling of negativity because it provides a temporary escape, thereby blocking out bad energies with a temporary feeling of wellbeing.

This negative spiral is a situation any of us could find ourselves gradually sinking into. When day after day is filled with stress and negativity, we return home to relax and unwind but soon find that the only way they block out all the negative vibes is to drink to oblivion. The next day we return to work for more, and then home again to drink. Over time, this builds up and creates both mental and physical illness.

Drinking to excess on a regular basis is very bad because it lowers our energy vibrations. It's a well-known fact that heavy drinking causes depression. This is especially true if we drink heavily on a regular basis and even more true if we are surrounded by negative energies when not drinking. Effectively, we put ourselves in a position whereby our energy levels are constantly drained.

"Three things cannot be hidden:
the sun, the moon and the truth."

Buddha

Just as it is possible to thrive in a positive cycle, the opposite of this is also true and that is, once one negative event has entered into our life, it is easier for another to enter, so that we become susceptible to attack by a second negative event, and then a third, and so on. Over time, the more negativity we absorb, the lower our vibrations become, making us more susceptible to more negative vibes. The problem arises when the balance tips and negative events start to dominate our life. Slowly, what happens is that we stop being able to differentiate between happy and sad because we become too numb to notice. We just carry on because everything starts to feel the same. This continual state of negativity and depression makes us susceptible to more negativity, and eventually this becomes a downward spiral. If this situation is allowed to continue unnoticed or ignored, it becomes the perfect environment for *"catching negativity"*.

Catching Negativity

Anyone who catches negativity will find themselves facing one disaster after another. It means loss, turbulence, destruction, and life goes in an ever downward spiral of negative vibration, or misery.

Over the years, I have seen a number of clients who have come to me at the end of their tether feeling that their lives have hit rock bottom. They are inundated and overwhelmed by problems they believe they have no control over, and there is no longer a sense of perspective. My guess is that you will know someone this has happened to.

There are an infinite number of external triggers: bankruptcy, divorce, personal insecurity, broken relationships, poor physical health. The problem for so many of the clients I see is that they so feel overwhelmed, they do not know what to do or where to start. I see many people in this frame of mind. On many occasions, I am the first and only person who is "let in" on the secret.

I repeat the point I made earlier that positive thoughts liberate us, negative thoughts inhibit us. It is vital that we learn how to manage our thinking so that we can manage our lives.

"Holding onto anger is like holding onto a hot coal
with the intent of throwing it at someone else:
you are the one who gets burned."

Buddha

Tuning our innate sixth sense into positivity is wonderfully empowering, but just doing this alone isn't always enough. In other words, we have to be able to recognise external sources of negativity and have the coping strategies to deal with them to manage our lives before we sink to the level whereby we lose control and have no idea where to start.

I cannot stress enough how damaging negative energies are and how important it is to keep our energies grounded and focused in the positive. We should always be vigilant to recognise those things outside ourselves that are not good for us.

Power of Affirmations

Affirmations are a wonderful way of regaining control and empowering ourselves. Affirmations are short statements that are repeated several times a day for a period of time. Over simplified as it may seem, affirmations can really help us to turn our lives around.

There are many fabulous affirmations, too many great ones to repeat here. You may like to source a book dedicated to this subject. The point I want to make here is that affirmations really work. They are incredibly powerful and work brilliantly to help us turn our lives around.

"All who call on God in true faith, earnestly from the heart, will certainly be heard and will receive what they have asked and desired."

Martin Luther King

Listening to Our Feelings

A valuable short hand way of being vigilant about what we draw towards ourselves is to listen to our feelings. Feelings are instinctive in each of us. It is these instincts that have enabled us to survive through the process of evolution.

Feelings tell us exactly what our thoughts are as instantaneous emotions. Listening to our feelings enables us to tell whether something is good or bad for us. These feelings feed back into our thoughts, enabling us to protect ourselves.

We are all innately programmed to read our own feelings and to some extent, the feelings of those around us. We are all innately vibe sensitive. In our increasing trend to be "image conscious" and "civilised", we have forgotten how to connect to this sense inside ourselves.

Vibe Sensitive

I pick up vibes from people, especially negative ones, very quickly. Since being a small child, I have been able to sense auras and sound around people and objects as well as things around me, whether I like it or not. This is not only true with physical people and spirit, it is also true with situations in general. For example, I can walk into a building and suddenly realise I have to get out quickly. This exact same thing happened years ago when my son was a small boy and my husband and I took him to a burger bar as a treat. Shortly after ordering the meal, I had a terrible overwhelming feeling and knew that something was going to go badly wrong. Reluctantly, my husband agreed to leave and we ate our food in the car. Later that day, the news reported that a gunman had gone into the same burger bar chain and opened fire on innocent people at the same time I felt the need to leave.

Just like when I was a little girl and saw my dead brother, there is, of course, a moral dilemma here: do you tell? And, if so, who do you tell? And, if you do tell, will you be believed or locked up as a suspect? It's a tricky one. Suffice here to say that I could quote many examples, but the point is the same: these energies are all around every one of us and we are all innately capable of picking up these vibes if we so chose. But, we have to allow it to happen, and that means not only listening to our feelings but hearing the thoughts they create inside us. It is the combination of feelings and the thoughts they create inside us that have enabled us to evolve. Most of us have either forgotten how to do this or chose not to listen to our inner voice. In effect, we have tuned ourselves out in preference to an apparently more sophisticated lifestyle. However, we will always originate from divine source, and therefore, will always be able to tune in if we try.

"Let us not love in word, neither in tongue; but in
deed and truth."

John 3:18
(King James Bible)

Protecting Our Energy

The work I do brings me into contact with all sorts of people from every walk of life. As I mentioned, when people come to see me for the first time, they come for a specific reason, usually in search of answers to a specific problem after something has gone wrong in their life. By their very nature, problems are negative. When clients leave my office after a reading, they also leave their negative energy behind them. In fact, sometimes after a client has left, I can walk back into my office and see that the atmosphere in the room is cloudy.

Potentially, I am constantly in a position where I may be exposed to the negative vibes of others. It is therefore vital to spend a few minutes every day focusing on my own positive thoughts so I can attract positive energies towards me. Negativity cannot attack us if we stay focused in the positive. Negativity can only get to us if we allow our energies to become low or diluted.

I strongly believe that negativity is a modern disease that we are all susceptible to. We all have the *free will* to choose whether to stay inside a negative loop or change our lives. I have seen many clients completely turn their lives around over the years through extremely difficult circumstances.

One of my regular clients told me that I had helped a friend of hers turn his life around. This man, a strong looking man in his late 20's, turned up at my office and sat opposite to me almost grudgingly, and very tetchy. Aside from his gruff exterior, I picked up that he was a very sensitive man who was deeply troubled by personal issues. I was able to relay pertinent information to him about these matters that only he could have known. I also picked up that the problems around him were creating serious stress and affecting his mental health. There was a sense of relief in him because he knew that the information I had given him was correct. He then felt he could open up to me so that we were able to consider some options to move him forward. It was as though I was the first person he had talked to about the negativity around him, and that he had bottled up all this inner tension, keeping it to himself. This man arrived as a complete sceptic and left a believer and two inches taller.

I gather from my regular client source, who was friends with this man, that it was his intention to take his own life. Simply by confiding in another human being, and being shown that his way of thinking was working against him, he was able to completely turn his life around. Once he was able to gain a sense of perspective and understand that he had to think differently, he was back in control of his life.

Another client who came to see me once was clearly suffering with anorexia nervosa as she was extremely thin. I sensed that her body energy vibrations were dangerously low and that if she didn't act, she was in serious trouble which was threatening her life. The same information was echoed in her card spread. I had no option other than to tell her truthfully that she herself was endangering her own life and asked her directly, though kindly, why she believed she wasn't good enough and had to be so thin. She burst into tears and told me everything. Once again, I was the first person she had spoken to about this matter. Despite being surrounded by a loving family, she had chosen to bottle up all her problems and keep them secret as she was too ashamed to tell anyone. Once everything was out in the open we were able to talk about her sense of perspective and that the way she was thinking was working against her.

Often, when people experience problems they go into denial and battle on in secret. This is very dangerous for our mental wellbeing. Left unchecked, some problems grow and so do the negative thoughts that accompany them. Many people simply do not possess the coping strategies to turn their lives around because they have never given themselves the chance to learn the skills.

So many of the clients who come to see me, feel stuck, alone and very afraid. For anyone who may feel overwhelmed and imprisoned in dense mental fog, one immediate escape route is to **tell someone.**

"The secret of change is to focus, not on fighting the old, but on building the new."

Socrates

The Power of Positive Thinking

I have been practicing positive thinking and meditation for more than thirty years. Over the years, my ability to tap into positive energy has become stronger. This is reflected in every area of my life, especially when I read for clients

When I look back, it seems to me that ability to tune in has grown and developed through different stages. Sometimes, I have been exposed to the same lesson several times before being able to move forward to the next.

I have literally "grown into" a way of thinking that has had phenomenal repercussions on the quality of my life.

Every day, at least once, I focus on all the good things in my life. When I do this, I *know* that my thoughts are being listened to and that the universe will respond. I have no doubts about this at all. When we really *know* this, it is the most liberating and empowering feeling in the world. *Knowing* the phenomenal power and impact our thoughts have outside ourselves changes everything. Even so, it has taken me a long time to train my mind to accept all these truths. I can only say the benefits are miraculous.

At one time I used to worry about if I could pay my bills, like everyone. Not anymore. Now I never worry as I *know* I am not alone on life's journey. I have such faith in the power of universal love, and believe that this is energy is God.

"I believe that I am always divinely guided.
I believe that I will always take the right turn off the road.
I believe that God will always make a way where there is no way."

Emerson

CHAPTER FIVE

EARTH-BOUND AND SPIRIT-BOUND ENERGY

"Apathy and evil. The two work hand in hand.
They are the same, really...
Evil wills it. Apathy allows it.
Evil hates the innocent and the defenseless most of all.
Apathy doesn't care as long as it's not personally inconvenienced."

Jake Thoene

In the last chapter, we explored how to identify and guard against negativity outside our own thought space, that is, from external sources such as the relationships and events around us in our daily lives. I do not believe that any of us are born "evil". We can all stray off the pathway into negative zones. That's life. To continue unguarded along this pathway is very dangerous for us because eventually, we can unwittingly invite negative *spiritual* energy or attachments towards us.

As we have established, thoughts have phenomenal power in shaping our lives. Our thoughts are living energies in the universe, and our dominant thoughts *always* come back to manifest themselves in our lives, whether or not we are consciously trying to make this happen. The key to empowerment is being vigilant both about what we allow ourselves to think, and who and what we allow into our lives.

Our own thought processes and the external environment we allow to be influenced by are two sources of negative energy that I call *"earth-bound"* negative sources, as they come from fellow human beings and the knock on effects of human action.

However, there is another source of negativity that I would like to explore with you, and that is "spirit-bound" negativity.

I have come across spirit-bound negativity at several junctures in my career.

Earth-bound and Spirit-bound Negativity

Earth-bound negativity, that is, the negativity that comes from fellow human beings, is only minute compared to what is out there as the force of negative energy in the universe.

As we have explored, earth-bound negativity comes directly or indirectly from the thoughts, actions and behaviours of people.

Everything we do has its origins in thought. Actions and behaviours follow on from thoughts not the other way around. Similarly, earth-bound negativity always stems from the seeds of negative thought. Whenever we allow the seeds of any negative thought to grow, we enable the negative energy inside ourselves to grow.

By allowing ourselves to dwell on a small negative idea, say a niggling feeling of resentment or jealousy that we cannot let go of, we enable the idea to grow. If unchecked, it will become a dominant thought pattern. The next stage is that these thoughts are then acted out as nasty behaviours, like lying, deliberately causing trouble for others, dramatic attention seeking, and so on.

Once negative energy becomes self-perpetuating and starts to thrive, it can quickly mushroom into wilful nastiness. This is the perfect situation for spirit-bound negativity to draw itself into this energy cycle.

At an individual level, the more negative thoughts and energy a person invests in, the more negative attachments they attract. These attachments grow and get stronger over time, thereby inviting still more negative entities. As we will explore, I have witnessed this situation for myself several times in my career. I believe that negative spirit-bound energy is a form of attachment from souls who are on a lower level. You don't have to be a murderer to be on this lower level: *you descend to this level slowly starting with the seeds of negative ideas.*

> "We are what our thoughts have made us;
> so take care about what you think.
> Words are secondary.
> Thoughts live; they travel far."
>
> Swami Vivekananda

Spirit-bound Energy and Negative Attachments

As we have explored, a person who perpetually participates with negative thoughts, such as jealousy, spitefulness, nastiness, and so on, is doomed to live in a negative loop, until such times as they acknowledge their thought processes and behaviours, and make a conscious effort to change them.

Whenever people open themselves up to bad thoughts and behaviours, they are inadvertently inviting spirit-bound negativity or negative attachments.

All of us are susceptible to think negative thoughts from time to time. However, *perpetual* negative thought patterns and exposure to negative people and situations can be extremely damaging. Be very careful: negative spirit-bound energy needs earth-bound negative energy to attach to.

I try at all times to be vigilant about negative thinking and behaviour. Whenever anyone hurts or upsets me, I try never to hold onto the bad feeling of hurt or anger, etc. Instead, I always try to turn the negative into a positive by saying thank you for the lesson.

"Whenever evil befalls us, we ought to ask ourselves,
after the first suffering, how we can turn it into good.
So shall we take occasion, from one bitter root,
to raise perhaps many flowers."

Leigh Hunt

I have read for thousands of people over the years. Every client who leaves my office also leaves their energy behind them.

Sometimes when people visit me, they bring with them the energies of people who have passed over. Several times, I have seen the outline of a spirit standing next to a client. On one occasion, I actually saw smoke emit from the client's arm, gradually building into the outline of someone who couldn't quite materialise. The point is that I always take a few moments to ground myself after a client leaves. Every time I read for a client, I say a prayer after they have left. These prayers are to help both the client and the souls they bring with them. I also pray for myself so that I can remain protected from spirit-bound negativity and stop any negative attachment onto me. In fact, I have a Prayer of Protection hanging on my wall to keep me firmly rooted in divine positive energy, or God. (The reference for this prayer can be found in the reference section at the back of this book.)

It is vital in a job like mine to be constantly aware of negative energy. My home can sometimes be a busy place and it isn't an unusual occurrence for us to share our home with several uninvited guests!! I regularly witness spirit-bound energy in my home. I often see orbs floating around in my office and many times when I have been cooking in the kitchen, I see figures of people passing by the doorway. On a couple of occasions, clients have told me that heavy objects have lifted off the desk when I have gone out of the room. A few times when I have been drifting off to sleep, I have been able to hear spirits having a conversation. On one occasion, the conversation went on for so long that I have had to tell them off so that I could get to sleep.

Thankfully, there are few examples of spirit-bound negativity looking for opportunities for attachment in my home.

There is one particular spirit, a woman, who has tried numerous times to get me to notice her. Several times now, she has simply appeared literally in my face, so close and so sudden that I was taken aback momentarily. It is important to stay strong and grounded in positive belief in such times. I have had to be very firm and tell her, as I have told others:

"Go away. There is nothing greater than God. Now go away and leave me alone."

A similar thing has happened on a couple of other occasions where spirit-bound negativity has looked more forcefully for opportunities to attach to me or my family. On both these occasions, illness was involved.

The first incident happened shortly after my husband was diagnosed with a lung disease. All evening, the dog was unusually restless and at 2am, came to wake me, then ran downstairs barking. Two hours later, he did the same thing. As he had never behaved like this before, I knew something was wrong, so I followed him downstairs. As soon as my foot hit the bottom step, the electricity tripped and the lights went out. There was no sign of any intruder so I went back to bed. As I lay down, I sensed a very strong, angry energy was with us in the room. I kept calm and knew that if I stayed focused on God, it, whatever "it" was, could not attack me or my husband. Suddenly, the blinds started moving so I started to pray out loud. With that, "it" became angrier. The more I prayed, the angrier it got, and the more the blinds rattled. I continued to pray, until "it" eventually stopped. As with other spirit-bound energies, I have no idea where or why this spirit-bound energy came from, why it was so angry or where it went.

"Nobody can hurt me without my permission."

Mahatma Gandhi

How Negativity Affects Us

I believe there was negative energy around the house that night that caused the dog to fret and the lights to trip. Whatever was in the room with us that night was a strong, angry energy. It must have been strong to move the blinds so aggressively!

It is important to see the motivation of spirit-bound negativity is to intimidate, dominate, and throw us off course so it can survive: negativity breeds on negativity. As long as we believe in the positive, divine energy or God, there is nothing to fear. There is literally nothing good in negative energy. It is an entirely bad energy that will cause disruption, unhappiness, misery, depression, illness, and so on.

"Darkness cannot drive out darkness; only light can do that.
Hate cannot drive out hate; only love can do that."

Martin Luther King

There is one particular negative spirit who has come to me when I feel weak and drained.

It started when I really didn't feel well. I had a very high temperature and was in a lot of pain, so went to bed, obviously on a lower ebb than usual. As I lay there, I sensed something approaching me, so I turned to look.

Instead of seeing the room, I saw a semi opaque film covering my eyes and face that felt soft, but I could not touch my skin. Then suddenly, a man's face appeared outside this barrier. He kept trying to press his face onto mine. Instinctively, I knew that this man was negative spirit-bound energy and that he shouldn't be near me, so I told him off with the usual:

"Go away. There is nothing greater than God. Now go away and leave me alone."

He jumped away from me as though he was shocked that I had seen him. I turned over and carried on trying to sleep, but he approached me again, and I sensed a heavy oppressive sensation on the side of my head. Once again, I told him to go away, more firmly this time, and then as I lay in bed, I started to pray. As I continued, I saw him gradually retreat away from me.

My son has also seen this man in our home. We both believe he is a negative spirit-bound entity looking for attachment.

Gradually lost souls like this who are able to attach themselves, bring negativity into the life of the person they attach to bringing illness, bad luck, misery, and so on.

"There are dark shadows on the earth,
but the lights are stronger in contrast."

Charles Dickens

Often, negative attachments become multiple, so that once one negative attachment has latched onto a person who is ill or going through a bad phase in their life, it is easier for other negative attachments to hook onto us and feed off us and we may experience one bad event after another. This is another way we can catch negativity: as more and more things go wrong in a person's life, it becomes harder and harder to maintain a sense of focus and balanced optimism until we start to forget what happiness or enjoyment is. This is precisely the sort of trigger that may invite someone to drink to excess, or turn to drugs to block these seemingly endless bad feelings. These conditions are the perfect breeding ground for earth-bound negativity, and spirit-bound attachments in particular.

"If I have the gift of prophecy and can fathom all mysteries and all knowledge and if I have faith that can move mountains, but have not love, I am nothing."

Corinthians 13.2
(New International Version)

Unhealthy drink and drug use enables us to believe that we are releasing negative feelings and moods, but inadvertently, we are lowering our vibrations or energies, making ourselves even more vulnerable, thereby enabling even more negativity to creep in. Often when people drink to excess, especially those who drink to oblivion on a regular basis, display quite noticeable personality changes, so while they are intoxicated, they become different people. This is exactly the scenario I am talking about.

Gradually, as more things go wrong, we may start to feel more and more depleted until we experience a sense of detachment and helplessness to change things. Over time, this negativity spirals even further down until the person reaches lower and lower levels, whereupon they may begin to experience extreme mental strain or even a serious illness, like alcoholism, drug addiction or clinical depression.

I strongly believe that clinical depression is caused by perpetual multiple negative attachments, both earth-bound and spirit-bound. I firmly believe it is possible to *catch negativity* and that *this is one of the main axes or root causes of emotional illness.*

I cannot emphasise enough how dangerous negativity is if you do not guard against it. You can only do that if you know what negativity is and how it manifests itself in the family, friends and events that surround us. Often, these events may appear to be out of our control. If this is the case, it is vital to ensure we guard ourselves from further negative attack by managing our thoughts through our feelings.

Managing our thoughts so that they are predominately positive ones is vital, not only to enable us to live a more fulfilling life, but to guard ourselves against the kind of negative attack I have described; evil cannot reign where there is love. Each light in this world, no matter how small, is a light to get rid of the darkness.

"Every minute you are thinking of evil,
you might have been thinking of good instead.
Refuse to pander to a morbid interest in your own misdeeds.
Pick yourself up, be sorry, shake yourself, and go on again."

Evelyn Underhill

Whenever I read for a client, I am actively inviting and allowing their energies to pass through me so that I can give them information. This also applies to any spirit-bound energy that exists around a client. It isn't possible to filter which energies *I want* to come towards me from those I don't want. I am the link or the channel and my role is to pass on information to the clients who come to see me. No matter how I try, some of the negativity clients bring with them rubs off onto me. I cannot pass this energy back to the client who brings it, or indeed pass it onto any other client who comes to see me. This energy stays only with me. Clients who come to see me are never in danger of catching negativity from me, or the energies of others who have been before them. What I am saying is that because I am constantly dealing with peoples' problems and tuning into the energies surrounding them, I constantly have to be aware of negativity and negative attack, and protect myself against it. Always remember that negativity can only attack you if you let it. Thankfully, it is only once in my career as a clairvoyant that I have met a person who exuded negativity.

Exuding Negativity

It was several years ago now that I saw such a person standing right in front of me in my office. At that time, my office was upstairs away from the rest of family.

As the last client left, I called to the man in the waiting area and invited him to my office. I had never met him before but as soon as he walked through the door I felt immediately uneasy, in fact, my first thoughts were that he was dangerous and I kept sensing his hands around my throat. The feelings he created in me where overwhelming.

There was something overbearingly intense about his whole presence and the look in his eyes was ferocious, like he was burning with anger and aggression. The edginess and intense penetrating stare continued even after he sat down.

In spite of the fact that he was giving me the creeps, I continued the reading as I do for all my other clients, beginning, as I always do, by tuning into with significant names and dates around him. I tried to stay as calm as possible, but inside I have to admit, I was frightened of him.

I kept sensing the feeling of his hands around my neck, as though he was just waiting for the right moment to lunge forward at me. I can only describe the intuition inside me as utterly intense, and I could not ignore the feeling that he was ready and waiting to do me serious harm. He frightened me so much.

After several minutes, he seemed to settle down slightly and I continued the reading knowing that there was something very wrong and troubled with him. It wasn't easy to stay focussed and calm, but I tried. I told him that I could see Canada around him. I had no opportunity to listen to his voice as, until this point, he didn't actually say a word or mumble a sound, but when I mentioned Canada, he said that he was Canadian and had been living in Liverpool and that he had a flight back to Canada in the next two days. After this, he seemed to calm down. At least, that's what I thought. Later in the reading, I asked him if there were any questions he would like to ask me. Unbelievably, his first question was, *"Have you ever done a murderer before?"*

Even though I was terrified inside, I tried to maintain an air of calm and told him that I had done readings for people who have accidentally killed people, through car accidents and so on, and that in the last thirty years I had probably had fifteen or so families who had had relatives murdered, so yes, I had "done a murderer". The hypnotic stare and intensity returned to his eyes as well as his tone, *"But what happens to murderers? After they die, I mean?"*

Keeping as calm as possible, I explained that it really depends on the circumstances, for example, whether the murder was accidental, calculated, provoked, and so on. Even so, he repeated his question with the same malevolence.

At this stage, I tried to divert him by explaining how I saw my job. That I am not in a position to judge anyone, I am merely here to help people. The only judge is God. It didn't matter what I said, he was not going to be diverted from his question which he repeated, *"So what do **you** think happens to murderers when they die?"*

As we continued to talk, I rested my elbow on the table, and leaned my head on my hand, pretending I was relaxed and focussed on listening to him. Suddenly, I felt excruciating pain and sensed that I had been stabbed in my ear.

I immediately leapt out of my chair and screamed - something I don't normally do to my clients! He stood up and stared at me, then looked around the room anxiously. In that moment, I knew that he was as terrified as I was.

Suddenly, the atmosphere in the room became very thick and heavy, just the way it does before a thunder storm, and I sensed straight away that there was a very strong spiritual presence with us. Talk about an elephant in the room, you should try a spirit!

For several seconds the man in my office stared open mouthed in bewilderment. Secretly, I was as bewildered and scared as he was but tried not to show it. Instead, I tried to concentrate on the presence with us in the room. He nervously spluttered out, *"What's wrong, what just happened?"* Not wanting to alarm or provoke him in any way, I told him as calmly as possible that there was somebody with us in the room.

I have noticed several times in my career that in moments like these, there is an overwhelming calmness that comes over me, as though I am actively protected by powerful spiritual energy. Suddenly, his presence no longer bothered me as I felt very comforted by the spiritual presence in the room.

It was different for him! His forehead pealed back, his eyes widened like saucers and his mouth drooped open even more. For a few seconds, he was frozen to the spot. Then suddenly, with shaking hands, he found his inner strength, fumbled for the money from his pocket, threw it at the desk, made a hurried dash for the door, ran down the stairs and out through the front door as quickly as his legs would carry him.

"If you look into your own heart, and you find nothing wrong there, what is there to worry about? What is there to fear?"

Confucius

I felt rather sorry for him. I think I gave him the biggest scare of his life. It was never my intention to frighten him, but I have to say, he really frightened me.

He knew as well as I did that there was somebody with us in the room. I shall never know who it was for certain, but I have a very strong suspicion that he had done some very serious harm to someone and that the pain I felt was the pain he had inflicted on the spirit who was with us. I strongly suspect that it was this man's intention was to do harm to me if I picked up on the truth. I am also certain that the presence in that room protected me from being harmed by him. It wasn't a dark or negative energy, but protective, and powerful

As I have already said, I have noticed many times that I am protected. I strongly believe that this protection comes through the practise of tuning into divine energy through positive thinking. This incident happened many years ago before I understood the level of protection around me.

Marks of Spiritual Protection

The next day, I went for my usual Chinese acupuncture therapy session. I believe these sessions help to open up my meridian energies and boost my spiritual energy, as daily life sometimes creates energy blockages in our bodies. However, on this particular day, the therapist told me that he couldn't do my session as I had shingles all across my back. I had no idea about this until he told me. In fact, the shingles ran all the way from my forehead, past my ear and neck, exactly where I had felt the intense excruciating pain. The nervous shock that penetrated my eardrum was so powerful that it left shingles behind. I had never had shingles before this point, and I have never had shingles since – another reason why I keep the protection prayer in my office!

I have no idea whether this man was leaving for Canada because he was involved in a murder case, but the energy that came from him was very bad and unpleasant. Thankfully, I do not see many people like this!

> "It is easy to hate and it is difficult to love.
> This is how the whole scheme of things works.
> All good things are difficult to achieve;
> and bad things are very easy to get."
>
> Confucius

Never "Play" with Spirit

Before I start a reading, I spend several minutes just tuning into what is around the person in front of me.

I may be given significant names or dates of birthdays or anniversaries. This information comes to me as sound usually, and will repeat over and over until I pass that information on.

Some people can be so closed minded to the information they are being given from spirit through me. I have had a few clients say to me, *"Do you link with spirit?"*.

I wonder where they could think I could possibly have gleaned all this information from!

For anyone who thinks that "dabbling" in spiritual matters is a form of entertainment, I would strongly urge you to think again. *Never ever* play with spirit as you have no idea what you are opening yourself up to.

Our minds are the most phenomenally powerful attribute we possess but there also phenomenally powerful forces at work outside of us that are beyond our wildest dreams. *Never, never, ever, ever* underestimate negativity. It is an extremely damaging, dangerous energy and must be avoided at all costs. Negativity can make us vulnerable to negative attack and even susceptible to *catching negativity.* Both of these scenarios are very bad news.

Trust me when I say that you *must* be careful what you dabble with as it is easy to tap into the darker side without being fully aware of what you are taking on board. This is another reason why, doing the work I do, it is vital to keep humble and grounded.

"Just as a candle cannot burn without fire,
man cannot live without a spiritual life."

Buddha

CHAPTER SIX

COINCIDENCE

"Everything in the universe is composed of energy, or vibration.
The vibration of words is, by extension, a grossed expression
of the vibrations of thoughts."

Paramahansa Yogananda

Our way of thinking and the way we see ourselves in relation to the universe is the footing we build our lives on. Everything we do follows on from this, not the other way around. We are in control of our own lives, life is not in control of us.

Our thoughts are the most powerful thing we possess as they are alive in the universe and continually tuning us into like energy vibrations. Our dominant thoughts engage us in an energy loop so that the energy we send out through thought, comes back to manifest in our lives. This thought dialogue happens whether we are consciously aware of it or not.

For most of us, this innate ability remains untapped and underutilised, yet this magic exists inside and outside all of us, ready and waiting to be used to empower us. I can only do the job I do because I am in tune with this magic. Thoughts are our sixth sense, the sense we have forgotten we

have, but we can all make this sense work for us. Learning to tap into it properly has the potential to empower every area of our lives.

Once we make a conscious effort to tune in our thoughts, we are making a link to a very powerful energy source. Whatever we think, will come back to us. Sometimes, the manifestation of this can take years, sometimes days or even hours. But it will come back! Once the evidence shows up, our faith in the process increases, so we practise again, and this faith brings more faith, and so on.

> "When an idea exclusively occupies the mind,
> it is transformed into an actual physical or mental state."
>
> Swami Vivekananda

Thought Manifestation or Coincidence?

As I have already said, I have been tuning in to this source energy for so long now that my link to it is automatic and I am continually engaged in thought dialogue: I feed into it, and it feeds into me. This love-gratitude energy loop is on-going. There is nothing special about me. We can all tap into this magic through changing the way we think.

Years ago, like most people, I would have regarded the uncanny events that have happened to me as mere coincidence. Not now.

Over the years, there have been simply too many "uncanny" things happen to explain them away as merely coincidental. Often these "coincidental" events have literally fallen into my pathway in incredibly bizarre ways. It is my firm belief that these things come from my on-going communication with the love energy loop or positive thought. This continual thought dialogue is at the very centre of everything I do.

My ability to "see" and pick up information from a spiritual dimension, like names of people who have passed over, dates, places, and so on, is only a few steps away from this fundamentally simple process. In other words, this thought dialogue comes from the same source or dimension as the spiritual information I am able to impart to clients who come to see me. It's simply that I am more sensitive to tuning into these energies.

I know that I am only a conduit that another energy passes through. It isn't me at work when I give my clients readings, its source energy. This energy surrounds us all, therefore it is available to us all. If I were to regard myself as special in any way, I would not be able to tap into it. I am certain of that.

I have come to understand that the numerous "coincidental" events are not coincidental at all, but the result of applied positive thinking. In the magical process of thought, we unwittingly send out vibes and these "living thoughts" create scenarios whereby "coincidence" comes back to us. I would like to share a few examples to demonstrate this.

Christmas Presents

As Christmas approached one year, my son announced he wanted a TV, not the gift he had originally asked for and my husband announced that he would like a yellow canary in a cage, again, not the present he had originally asked for. As I had already bought their presents and didn't have any extra cash, there was no way this was going to happen before Christmas.

A few days before Christmas, I had a call from a regular client who was in very agitated state. She explained that she had found her ex-husband dead in his home. It was all very difficult for her, as he had been an abusive, and violent alcoholic husband, and she had decided to leave him. Even so, his death was a shock. To calm her down, I asked her what the background noise was. She told me it was a bird, a yellow canary in fact and she was looking for a home for it, did I know anyone?

She arrived at my doorstep on Christmas Eve with a yellow canary in a cage. She also said she had something else in the car for my son. I followed her to the car and watched as she pulled a TV from the back seat.

A yellow canary in a cage is a pretty unlikely coincidence, but combined with a TV set, it is very unlikely. Unconsciously, I had sent out this request through my thoughts. This is an example of what I mean about thoughts being living things. If you ask for something in your thoughts through positive energy, the universe will somehow give it back to you. This is the basis of the Law of Attraction, covered in *Esther and Jerry Hick's* brilliant books and others like *The Secret*. The law is that like attracts like, so whatever you ask for through thoughts is returned back to you as physical manifestation.

"Ask and it shall be given to you; seek, and you shall find;
knock and it shall be opened unto you:
for every one that asks will receive
and he that seeks will find,
and to him that knocks it shall be opened"

Matthew 7:7
(King James Bible)

The Mouli

After being diagnosed with breast cancer, a client of mine decided to do Gerson Therapy, an acclaimed, natural therapy for cancer and degenerative disease. To do the therapy properly, she needed to purchase a mouli or food mill and a salad spinner. These are very specific items. Short on cash, I told her to put out the thoughts for what she needed. Over the next few days, she did just this. Within a couple of weeks, she went into a charity shop and there, waiting on the bottom shelf of jumbled up bric-a-brac was a brand new mouli and a salad spinner. Both of these items still had shop labels on them and had never been used.

These two very simple examples show how channelling our thoughts can work to our advantage. Every one of us can do this. Whenever we want something, we simply have to focus on it clearly with positive thoughts. It is important to keep the request as simple as possible. Saying it helps to focus on it. Repeat the thought over and over. Wait for the thought you have sent out to materialise.

I would like to add a note of caution here. Many people make the mistake of thinking that they are asking for what they want, when in fact they are doing just the opposite and sending messages about what they don't want, or what is wrong. In other words, they focus on the negative aspects surrounding their desire, so their desire goes out as a negative, and of course, this is what they get back. If we want our thoughts to bring back the things we want, the thought must be happy, clear, and simple.

For example, let's suppose I need a specific item of clothing for a special occasion, say, a duck egg blue dress for instance. All my friends have been invited to the same event and require the same item of clothing. Whereas they can and do go right out and purchase what they need, at this particular point in time, I cannot afford a new dress, yet without it, I cannot attend the function. The most obvious way forward would be to send out the thought as a specific request, *"I need a duck egg blue dress for two weeks on Saturday."* Is this sufficient to bring the request into manifestation? The answer is no.

What is important in the delivery of the request is the energy or mindset that sends it: in spite of what I verbalise, my thought energy has to match the vibration of my request otherwise, my energies send out mixed messages. So, for example, as I send out the request "I need a duck egg blue dress for a week on Saturday" I may be resenting the fact that all my friends already have a dress or even that they can afford to buy a new dress. Whatever the scenario, the point is that the message

I am actually sending out is "This sucks, I haven't got a duck egg blue dress, and everyone else has, why me?" In other words, my request isn't a request but a resentment.

Am I going to see my request materialise? No, of course not. Whereas, if I send out the same request "I need a duck egg blue dress for two weeks on Saturday", and I *feel* grateful that I have been invited to a function with all my friends, and it is going to be a wonderful event, and so on. My dress will turn up some way or another because what I am actually *thinking and feeling* are vibes of happiness, pleasure, and gratitude. The dress is an incidental object in this process and so of course it will turn up if the request is sent with love and gratitude.

"According to your faith, be it unto you."

Matthew 9:29
(King James Bible)

These examples, where thought desires manifest themselves as physical objects, are only the very beginning of what exists in this ask receive loop. They may be very simple examples but they are very specific and demonstrate how thoughts can manifest in our lives if we specifically request them. The point is that we can ask for literally anything. No problem or difficulty is excluded. The more we practise or focus our thinking on what we want to attract, the more we attract.

Our thoughts really are alive, and like great magnets, pull back the same energy we send out. Thoughts don't just draw material objects towards us, they also activate emotionally significant events. I have witnessed this many, many times how our thoughts link us with a higher power in so many ways and at so many levels. I would like to share a few examples here.

The Poem by Anne Parker

While my mother was waiting for major heart surgery, I was very busy with work and unable to visit until after the operation. I had to ask a friend to buy a card that I rushed to write and send. I didn't have time to study the card or even read the verse inside it. However, my mother was delighted with the card, and asked if I had chosen it especially for her. I apologised that I hadn't read the verse, and that it was a friend, not myself who had chosen it. I was very surprised when I actually looked at it: on the front of the card was a poem entitled "Those who care it affects the heart", by Anne Parker. The message was significant not only because my mother was having a heart operation, but because Anne Parker was my Grandmother's name and she died fifteen years earlier. This gave my mother enormous comfort at a very difficult time and proved that her mother was around her.

Shortly before my mother died, I visited her in hospital and found her trying to write out another poem for a lady in the opposite bed. My mother was very sick, so I copied it for her. Shortly after this, my mother died.

A few months later, we had a family holiday in Malta. Pushing our son around in his buggy, I began to think about my mother and how much I missed her. Strolling into a gift shop to browse, I was amazed to see, hanging on the wall directly in front of me, the same poem she had tried to write out, the same one I copied. It wasn't a well-known poem and so I was totally shocked to see *that* poem of all poems in a gift shop, especially in a foreign country. A great feeling of inner peace and happiness washed over me as I realised my mother was around.

"I find hope in the darkest of days and focus in the brightest.
I do not judge the universe."

Dalai Lama

My Client Margaret

I have known some of my regular clients for many years. One such client was Margaret. Over the many years I saw her, she always insisted I should get out more and have a romance in my life. There was no one on the scene and I was simply too busy to make the effort myself.

Later that year, a Greek Orthodox Priest read my coffee cup and told me that there would be a man in my life very soon who would become my husband. I couldn't see this myself, and thought that what he said was rubbish. I little while later, I put out the thought, *making sure that my intention matched the vibration of my request*, that I was ready for and wanted a romance in my life. In other words, instead of resenting the fact that I didn't have a romance, I focused on my request with joy and invited it as I was ready.

A couple of weeks later, I had three telephone calls from a man who didn't know whether he wanted to come for a reading or not. His numerous calls started to drive me potty but eventually, he decided to come. I was doing a reading for another client when he arrived. While sitting in the waiting area, he lit up a cigarette. This man was certainly irritating!

When I started reading for him, I told him he was going to meet someone else and within eighteen months he would be married. I went on to ask about a lady called Margaret who was around him. He told me that Margaret was his Auntie who had recently died. As we talked, I realised it was *my* client Margaret.

I was right about this man marrying: twelve months later he was married. What I had failed to see was that it was *me* he would be marrying!

This is an example of what I mean by divine guidance and protection. I sent out the thought that I was ready for a man in my life and he literally turned up at the door. The fact he is related to my client Margaret was no coincidence either.

"Before the throne of the Almighty,
man will be judged not for his acts but by his intentions.
For God alone reads our hearts."

Gandhi

Lost Letters

Another example of spiritual protection and support was told to me by one of my clients. In a house move, a box of her treasured possessions, mainly letters from her late husband, went missing. She was very upset about this and often wished for them to turn up. More than two years later, a double quantity of logs was delivery to her home by mistake. This meant she had to reorganise the log shed, a job she hated. While tidying, she found the old familiar tatty cardboard boxes that she had moved several times, but this time, when she lifted the box, the contents spilled out onto the floor. Amid the bundle was her late husband's letters. What is curious in this story is that she had searched through this box many times before and never found the letters. Even more curious, this find happened the day before her fortieth birthday. These "uncanny" events were her very special birthday present.

"You can't connect the dots looking forwards;
you can only connect them looking backward.
So, you have to trust that the dots will
somehow connect in your future.
You have to trust in something
- your gut, destiny, life, karma, whatever.
This approach has never let me down,
and it has made all the difference in my life."

Steve Jobs

"Wrong" Train

Every thought really does count, and spiritual protection happens in very bizarre ways. This is demonstrated through the example of my client Gillian, who had to go to London for a meeting. Unusually on this particular morning, she found her usual local train station was closed. The next station was over thirty miles away so she had to drive literally miles out of her way. All day, her heart had been heavy and preoccupied with a man in her life who, for a period of time, had been acting strangely. He claimed this was due to work pressures, however, none of this felt right to Gillian who was heavy hearted. Sick of limbo land, she sent out the thought that she wanted to either be alone or together as a couple properly.

After a long day of meetings, she accidentally boarded the wrong train home: instead of the express service, she had boarded the slow train. This meant she would be over an hour late. She attempted to call home to say just this, but just as she dialled, her battery went dead. When she finally arrived back at the re-rooted train station to pick up her car, the last thing she expected to see right on the very same platform, was her partner locked in an embrace with another woman. Clearly, this may not have been the ideal solution she had hoped for, but in the long run, it helped her to know the truth and therefore move on. It is the combination of these events all together that make this story interesting: closure of the local train station; embarking on the wrong train home; her phone losing charge and the "chance" meeting. These unlikely combined events conspired together enabling her to find out the truth.

Coincidence and Spiritual Protection

Years ago, I would have regarded these kinds of examples as coincidental. Not anymore. Simply too many things of this nature have occurred and I have come to realise that coincidence alone cannot be the explanation.

The more I have channelled my thoughts, the more coincidence has come into my life. This goes way beyond the manifestation of physical things.

"Trust in the Lord with all your heart and lean not on your own understanding, in all ways acknowledge Him and He will make your path straight."

Proverbs 3:5-6
(New International Version)

I believe that there is a blurring or cross over between our thoughts being living entities in the universe and spiritual protection. To me, they are a progression along the same dimension because they come from the same source energy. In other words, though thought requests may well turn up as objects, there is a deeper, more spiritual manifestation that takes longer to come back to us, and that is spiritual protection. I believe the examples above are evidence of this spiritual protection in action and that whether we are aware of it or not, each of us is continually linking with a higher spiritual power through our thoughts.

We may begin our initiation into this thought dialogue loop at a very simple level, whereby we ask for physical things to manifest in our lives, but with practise, each of us can activate this protection. The more we practise and engage with the loop, the more magic we activate back into our lives. I have such faith and belief that my continual link through thought connects me to a higher power. I believe that through this power, I am always divinely guided and provided for.

Chapter Seven

Death and Bereavement

"Great men are those who see that spiritual is stronger
than any material force –
that thoughts rule the world."

Ralph Waldo Emerson

Everything we do, and everything we set out to achieve in our lives has its origin in our way of thinking, and the way we see ourselves in relation to the universe. We live out our lives from this central axis point. Through the constant interaction between our dominant thought vibrations with the universe, we attract back the same energy to manifest in our lives. Day on day, year on year, these interactions make up our lives.

Though these principles may seem oversimplified, they have much deeper and richer ramifications because if our thoughts make our lives, then our lives make our souls.

Thoughts Make Us

Everything in our lives comes from the way we think, not the other way around. Even though life may throw curved balls at us from time to time, life isn't making us, we make it by the way we respond to what happens to us. In this way, we have control because what we think is entirely our own choice.

Clients come to see me with all sorts of issues, but the root of most problems comes from negative thought patterns such as jealousy, resentment, obsessions with money, and self-image. One of the worst is wishing harm to others and even worse, acting out revenge.

This is all so wasteful and creates problems in our own lives as it imprisons us in this thought space. This is self-destructive. Not only do our dominant thoughts affect our lives, they also shape our soul.

"You have to grow from the inside out.
None can teach you, none can make you spiritual.
There is no other teacher but your own soul."

Swami Vivekananda

I repeat, *everything* comes from the way we think. Our dominant thoughts determine everything about us in our lives and afterwards, because it is exactly the same energy we use to shape our soul. Just as our thoughts only attract the same energy into our lives, our soul is pulled towards the same vibration of our dominant thought patterns after passing over. So, our soul is the sum total of all our thoughts.

Just as clients come to see me with personal problems, the other major reason to visit is to make contact with someone who has passed over. I have been a channel for spirit thousands of times over the years. If our soul didn't survive death, then there would be no spirit, and if there were no spirit, then I simply wouldn't be able to pass on the information I do. The details I have been able to impart to clients have repeatedly proved to me that there is a spiritual dimension beyond this earthly plane.

Through my work, I now believe that we are all on this earth dimension or physical plane to learn and help one another. Anyone who wilfully goes against this purpose, through acting out or wishing bad towards others, is not only creating negative vibes, but also damaging their own souls.

> "It has always been a mystery to me how men can feel themselves honoured by the humiliation of their fellow beings"
>
> Buddha

Shaping Your Soul

Through our thoughts, we gradually form our lives. Our lives are the fabric of our souls, so our souls can only be the sum total of all out thoughts. It is the energy of our dominant thoughts patterns, good, and bad, that we take with us after death. In other words, our thoughts shape our lives *and* our souls. In the same way that our thoughts are magnetic, so are our souls because after death, our soul is pulled to the same energy level as the vibe of our dominant thought patterns throughout our life.

Though our thoughts may be kept secret on the earthly plane, they cannot be hidden or kept secret in the spiritual dimension because our soul can only be drawn to its like energy.

There is no man with a white beard standing at the Pearly Gates with notes on a blackboard because there doesn't need to be. We are our own record.

From my years of experience, I am aware that there are different spiritual levels that we go to when we pass over. The things we do in our lives and the thoughts we think, determine the level we ascend to after our passing.

"Eye has not seen nor ear heard,
neither have entered into the heart of man,
the things that God hath prepared for them that love him"

Corinthians 2:9
(King James Bible)

Near Death Experience (NDE)

Research on Near Death Experiences (NDE), shows that the most common experience after actual physical death occurs is an overwhelming feeling of love from the universe. For many people, this feeling is accompanied by the huge shame and embarrassment of being selfish and not having done more to help humanity.

Often, people who encounter NDE return to an earthly state of living with a sense of humility and a desire to "do good" for fellow mankind.

There is not a single example of someone returning from NDE wishing they had a stainless steel fridge or a flat stomach!

"Happiness resides not in possessions and not in gold.
Happiness dwells in the soul."

Democritus

The Bonds of Love that Bind Us

The love that connects us while on the physical earthly plane does not vanish or diminish after we pass over. In fact, the longer we are alive on this earthly plane, the more it is familiar to us as "home" and therefore, we have a greater need to hang onto what we miss, especially our loved ones. We have a tendency to misunderstand and underestimate this while we are earth bound. The bonds of love work both ways: love ties us to spirit and spirit to us. In other words, spirit are just as tied to us as we are to them after death. Like our predominant thought energies, the love we have for our families and friends we take with us when we die.

I believe that the divide between this world and the spirit world is less for spirit to overcome than it is for us here on the physical earthly plane, as we overcomplicate what is fundamentally simple. In spirit there is only love. From my experience as a conduit, the love that passes through from spirit onto us becomes much stronger as it comes through the divine source energy.

In our everyday earthly lives, it is easy to forget about the bonds of love as we are continually side tracked by the struggles of daily life. However, it is very upsetting and worrying for our loved ones to see us grieving and suffering over their loss, especially when we may grieve for prolonged periods of time.

The Power of Love

I believe that it is extremely important to talk to those who have passed over, as they are with us, especially in the beginning. This helps us to grieve but it also helps to reassure our loved ones that we know they are around us and need not feel guilty about our suffering over them.

When clients come to see me after a loved one has died, I am sometimes able to make contact and comfort their grief through communicating a name or place or circumstances of death of a loved one. I will hear a name in my head. This will keep repeating until I have said it out loud to a client.

However, when not seeking the advice of a medium, most spiritual communication is much more subtle. Spirit cannot directly interfere in our lives but they are around us, especially in difficult times. For the most part, they do this unseen and unheard by the vast majority of us, though they do try to show us they are around us. The signs may be subtle ones, but it is important to watch for them.

"All differences in this world are of degree and not of kind because oneness is the secret of everything."

Swami Vivekananda

Communication Through Symbols

When I first started out as a clairvoyant, I noticed that spirit often communicated a message to me through the use of symbols, although it took me several years to realise this was the case. I now believe that symbolic association and understanding occurs at the start of clairvoyant development.

After all the years of doing the type of work I do, I am less reliant on symbols as I am more highly tuned. Even so, there is one particular symbol that still has an emotional legacy for me, and that is the appearance of birds. I have come to regard the "uncanny" appearance of birds, especially magpies, as a bad omen. Magpies really do give me the creeps as I now associate their appearance with death. For example, one evening as I approached the front door, there, quite out of the blue, was a dead magpie lying on the footpath. I immediately knew that someone had died or was going to die. Sure enough, shortly after walking through the front door, there was a phone call to say that a relative had died. Another time, while I was reading for a client, a bird flew down the chimney, flapped around the room, and eventually escaped through the window. I had a strong suspicion of what that meant! I was careful to tell the client to take extra care of himself. Within a couple of weeks, I found out this client had died suddenly of a heart attack.

"Nothing is so strong as gentleness and
nothing is so gentle as real strength."

Ralph W. Sockman

As I have progressed through my spiritual journey, birds have become less of a significant symbol of death. Now I am told if someone is going to die, usually through a sudden flash of understanding or heightened perception, and I just *"know"*.

Though symbolic association may be a lower level of clairvoyant perception, it is a short hand way our loved ones often use to communicate a message to us.

I always tell clients that if they want to communicate with a loved one who has passed over, to send out the thought and state clearly the sign they would like to be used. What is crucially important in this contact or communication is that when the specific sign appears to confirm spiritual presence, we *must* always be prepared to acknowledge it and say thank you.

Falling feathers are a very good place to start. Just the other day, a white feather literally fell down in front of my face. There were no windows or doors open and no one except myself was in the room. I simply reached out my hand and let the feather fall into my palm. This was definitely a sign of spiritual energy and protection, and so I was careful to show my gratitude and say my thanks out loud.

As we have explored, expressing thanks is a way of re-entering the cycle, thereby attracting more communication and protection back to us. With practise, this will attract other symbols that may have specific meaning, for example, the smell of a loved one's perfume, or the smell of their particular brand of cigarettes, and so on.

One of my clients was perplexed by the continual appearance of five pence pieces in her day to day life. These coins appeared not only in the most unlikely of places but also so continually frequently, it was becoming bizarre. Many people dismissed the presence of the 5p's as "mere coincidence". However, this wasn't coincidence at all. The five pence pieces were symbolic of spiritual energy and protection. What was also interesting, was that whenever she became especially down or depressed, the five pence pieces stopped appearing, sometimes for days or weeks at a time, only to reappear when her unusually blue mood evaporated. Now that my client is aware of what the five pence pieces symbolise, they have a special meaning to her whenever they appear.

Spirit don't ever come through to you if they don't want to. You can ask them to, but you cannot make someone come through to you if they do not want to. You cannot *force* spirit to do anything.

I believe we must always keep watch for signs from spirit, as they are always around and trying to show us love and reassurance, especially in difficult times. As well as symbols, some of these signs can take the form of dreams.

Messages Through Dreams

We all dream. However, there are certain types of dreams that cross a threshold and go beyond the realm of being simply dreams, because they inform us of details of a future event. Such dreams are commonly known as premonitions. I have had premonitions about world affairs twice in my career: the Lockerbie tragedy and Princess Diana's death. Thankfully, most of the premonitions I have had are to do with family and friends, and I am always forewarned of an imminent passing.

I always find premonitions tricky: what do you do with the information? Telling someone is not only ethically problematic, there is also the problem of incredulity and sensationalism. Also, putting ideas and words into the thoughts of others about very serious matters is, I believe, morally wrong.

This was the case with some close relatives in the family. One evening, I had a dream about a family member's death. I telephoned to casually enquire that everything was well. A few days later, I had the same dream, but instead of phoning for a second time, I dismissed the dream and ignored my intuition. A few days later, I had a call to say my relative had died. I felt very guilty for not picking up the phone for a second time. To make matters worse, I wasn't able to attend the funeral. These two things together bothered me hugely.

A couple of weeks later while I was standing at the cashier's desk in the bank, I turned to look at an irritating figure hovering at my side. I gasped to see my dead relative standing at my side smiling at me. This was the last thing I expected! He stayed by my side with a reassuring smile for a several seconds. In those moments, I somehow knew that he understood. After this I didn't feel guilty anymore.

As I have said before, spirit do not come through to us if they do not want to. We can ask them to but we cannot make it happen. We cannot make spirit do anything they do not want to do, so if they do not want to come through, they won't.

"Believers look up, take courage.
The angels are nearer than you think."

Billy Graham

I now believe that life and death are indivisible as they are part of the same eternal loop. Life, not death, is the basic principle of the universe where everything is deathless. Death is simply a separation of the soul from the body.

As I now know for certain, life does not end after death. Of course, this doesn't stop grief and sorrow, but is does make the loss of a loved one less painful. Just because we cannot see our loved ones in the physical plane doesn't mean they do not exist. Loved ones who die are often nearby and usually draw near to us for mutual comfort.

"God sometimes does try to the uttermost those whom he wishes to bless."

Mahatma Gandhi

Chapter Eight

A Test of Faith

"The power of thought, for good or ill,
derives from the thought essence of the universe…
you do not realise the power of God that is in your mind."

Paramanhansa Yogananda

I hope by now that the phenomenal power of thought and the way we view ourselves in relation to the universe is evident.

Thoughts and our way of thinking are the fundamental building blocks of everything we do, not only because they affect everything we say and do, but also because they link us with phenomenally powerful like energies outside ourselves.

Thoughts are our innate sixth sense. Learning to tune into this sense is a skill that, like any other skill, comes with practise. Every thought really does count, and managing our thoughts has the potential to completely enrich our lives. *Knowing* that the universe is listening and responding is extremely empowering in itself, but once the evidence of this belief comes to manifest and positive changes take effect, know that this is only the starting point.

It has taken me a long time to train my mind and put all my faith and trust in this process. There have been a couple of times in my life when I have had doubts and felt betrayed by my own beliefs.

A Slap in the Face

I would have liked nothing better than to have had lots of children. Unfortunately, I have had many of problems over the years. My husband and I have lost four babies: a set of twins due to miscarriage and two ectopic pregnancies.

I was very upset and angry when I had my first ectopic pregnancy and lost my baby, but I was even angrier that I had no warning or preparation for the trauma. Up until this point, I had always felt very in tune with events like this and knew when something major was going to happen. On this occasion, however, I had no warning and I really couldn't understand this and was deeply shocked and upset to the point where I felt angry and betrayed. Not only did I lose the baby, the ectopic was also severely life threatening for me and had a dramatic effect on my future fertility.

Sometimes the best response to negativity is to cry it out of our system.

"Tears are often the telescope by which men see far into heaven."

Henry Ward Beecher

Once I had released this energy for a couple days, I woke up one morning and felt healed. Normally, people take six to eight week to recover from this type of operation. I was back at work within a week. I will come back to this point.

After the awful experience of the ectopic pregnancy, some years passed and I discovered I was pregnant once more.

I was absolutely over the moon and everything seemed to be progressing as it should.

My Worst Nightmare

One morning I woke up with an overwhelming feeling of dread convinced that I was having another ectopic in spite of the fact I had no symptoms. Three days later, a scan confirmed this and I needed emergency surgery.

I was absolutely devastated when I woke up to discover that not only had my remaining tube been removed, but I had also lost my baby. The mental anguish of those three days, knowing this would happen, yet knowing there was nothing I could do about it was almost unbearable.

"I think only through suffering,
all our wonderful human qualities come out in us.
Unless and until you suffer,
how will you understand other's suffering?"

Sree Chakravarti

I was very ill following the operation and then began to suffer with breathing difficulties. I was also grieving over my fourth lost baby and the realisation that I could never be pregnant again.

By this point I was angry. Having one life threatening ectopic was bad enough, but this second blow pushed me to the brink of emotional devastation. If anything was going to destroy my faith, then these combined events had the potential to do just that. I felt cheated and robbed. Worse, I felt betrayed by my own beliefs. After years of working for others free of charge in freezing cold churches, travelling miles at my own expense, living in grotty bedsits with no material possessions, this was how I was repaid? The thing I wanted most was taken from me. I was angry, devastated and confused. I sobbed until exhaustion took hold and I finally went to sleep.

"The guardian angels of life sometimes
fly so high as to be beyond our sight,
but they are always looking down upon us."

Jean Paul Richter

I woke to see a nurse standing at the side of the bed dressed in a dark blue uniform. She was quite plump with blonde hair and large round glasses. She exuded an inner beauty and calmness that made me feel totally serene and so safe. She leaned towards me, took my hand and just smiled. The peace and reassurance she instilled in me bowled me over with overwhelming love, and in those moments any anger I had, simply left me and I just knew not to question. She stood there like this for a little while, and we began to chat. She explained that I didn't have any blood clots and that my lungs would get better quickly. She kept reassuring me there was nothing to worry about and my stitches would heal within a couple of days. She then explained that she was going to get me up and out the bed, take the bag from my side and that I would be walking by the end of the day. I protested that I really didn't feel well and didn't want to get up yet. Suddenly, the curtain around the bed was pulled back and another nurse asked me who I was talking to. I pointed to the blonde haired nurse but when I looked to where she had been standing, she had vanished. I tried to figure out what was happening and then realised that she couldn't have been standing where I thought she was, as there was a bedside cabinet there instead. I also realised that as she had been talking, I hadn't seen her mouth move. She had communicated to me through her thoughts.

Whatever she was and where ever she came from, I felt that she healed me when I was at my lowest ebb and gave me a very special message that validated my beliefs. This feeling was communicated to me in such an overwhelmingly way, I cannot, and could not doubt. Somehow, I knew I already understood this and always had. I may not understand why I lost those babies, but I know that my beliefs and faith had not betrayed me.

"But if these beings guard you,
they do so because they have been summoned by your prayers."

Saint Ambrose

Just as this nurse had predicted, I started to heal very quickly. Also, everything she told me was medically correct.

By six o'clock I was walking. Within a week, I was back at work. Once again, my recovery was miraculous.

More than twenty years later, I firmly believe that these events were a test, not only of my own emotional strength, but of my own faith. Instead of destroying my beliefs, these events only served to make them stronger as they reinforced what I already knew to be the case. Indeed, I knew that I had always known.

The other major lesson it taught me was to never question why: why these things happened and why I wasn't forewarned. I now put all my faith and trust in the divine energy and I do not question.

"God will not look you over for medals, degrees or diplomas,
but for scars."

Elbert Hubbard

Faith in My Own Beliefs

Hindsight is a wonderful thing! It has taken a long time for me to more put all my faith and trust in this process. It has taken an equally long time for me to accept the signs of support and protection without cynical questioning that there is nothing more than "mere coincidence" at work.

The more we allow our faith to open up and grow, the more faith proves itself. I now pick up much more information for clients as I believe I am now easier to use as a channel. This is because I am more open and less cynical and sceptical about "proof". I no longer need proof; I just accept what I am shown without question.

Spiritual Activity in My Home

There is a lot of activity in our family home and we are all aware of it. In spite of my reassurances that we are protected through our beliefs my husband who was once very sceptical about spiritual matters, will now only go to bed with the lights on. In fact, if he is upstairs alone he always has *all* the lights on. Our son has grown up with these activities and isn't phased by it at all. He will frequently turn all the lights off that my husband has turned on. That's the way we live now, its normal - at least to me, if not to my husband!

Christmas Eve

One example of this that really warmed my heart concerns a man I helped a few times many years ago. He was an elderly chap called Sydney who slipped on the ice outside my house one cold winter's morning. This incident was the start of my friendship with Sydney who I knew only in the last years of his life.

Many years later, on Christmas Eve and I was wrapping presents and suddenly saw a flash of light. Assuming it was something on TV, I continued pottering. I stepped back to see Sydney sitting in the armchair. Usually, when I see spirit, I see a quick flash on and off for a few seconds. Not this time. Sydney sat in the chair for ages and he was absolutely solid like any physical person is. He didn't speak but I watched in amazement as he smiled at me. It was a lovely warm smile, and his aura filled the room with love. I watched Sydney for several minutes before going upstairs to wake my husband and tell him to come and see my old friend Sydney for himself.

My husband wasn't quite so keen. Over the years, I have had so many visitors that my husband no longer needs proof either!

"Every natural fact is a symbol of some spiritual fact."

Emerson

Positive Energy Flow

I have noticed many times that the office where I do most of my readings has a great deal of positive spiritual energy.

I sincerely believe that there is something other than me working with me and helping me when I come into my office. No matter how tired I am, I can give a client a reading in my office and give them huge amounts of energy.

I know this energy doesn't come from me: the energy somehow comes around me when I am in my office and passes through me to others. It is my belief that this energy comes through my on-going link into the positive thought dialogue loop. I am constantly in the presence of client energy. This energy is often negative or draining, and is left behind when they walk out through the door. No matter how bad their stories, I concentrate on gratitude as a form of healing energy for my clients and protection for myself.

The more we tune ourselves into the vibes, the more we get back. A simple two-step process of acknowledging all the positives and saying thank you, even for the smallest things, is the way to open up the energy cycle. In this way, the cycle will perpetuate itself and life quickly takes on a new direction.

This is my belief and it is unshakeable because it works!

Chapter Nine

The Perpetual Cycle

---

*"Don't you know that you yourselves are God's temples
and that God's spirit lives in you?"*

Corinthians 3:16
(Holman Christian Standard Bible)

Throughout this book, we have explored the phenomenal powers available to us through the way we think.

These powers are not separated from us on some unreachable moral high ground, but integrally part of every one of us to call on at any time to use to our advantage. This is because we all originate from source energy, so we are part of it and it is part of us. We can link back into source energy at any time by thinking thoughts that match the same vibration.

Our thoughts are the invisible thread that ties us to where we ultimately all belong. Tremendous gifts are bestowed on us through this invisible connection and take our abilities as human beings way **Beyond the Five Senses** we believe we are limited to. Thoughts are our sixth sense, and this gift is something we all possess.

For most of us, however, this gift is either underutilised or completely ignored, and we mistakenly believe we are passive travellers on a journey of life. So many of us end up going with the flow and focusing on what is wrong, not what is right.

Most of the people who come to see me, come for a specific reason, usually to shed light on a problem. Often, they feel trapped in a cycle they feel powerless to get out of. What they often cannot see is that their way of thinking is working against them not for them.

I hope by now it is clear that if we want our lives to work for us rather than being the victim to circumstance, it is vital that we manage our thoughts, especially our negative thoughts. Negative thoughts are the biggest obstacle blocking us from using of our innate gift or sixth sense. Proper use of our sixth sense connects us to the magic outside ourselves and has the power to enable us to transform our lives.

Life is not controlling us, we are controlling it. The starting point of this control comes from how we allow ourselves to think. As we have explored throughout this book, every thought really does count. There is a direct relationship between the energy vibration of our thoughts and the energy we link with outside ourselves in the universe. By deliberately managing our thinking we can tune our sixth sense into the magic outside ourselves and enrich our lives for the better.

Thought management requires minimal effort, yet, the results are miraculous. The way we think and the way we view ourselves in relation to our existence in the universe is the most fundamental key to our existence because it is the core of everything else we are.

Every thought we think has a vibration and creates an energy wave that the universe can read, even the ones we think are private secrets! Our dominant thoughts link us into an energy loop, and we enter into a thought dialogue connection. Our thoughts are like huge magnets, so whatever we think is attracted back to us. In this way, our thoughts are alive in the universe.

The powers available to us through our thoughts are remarkable. It is how we choose to direct our consciousness that is the key, because our dominant thoughts determine the energy loop we engage with.

Directing and managing our thoughts involves a very simple two-step process: first, identify all the positives in life and, two, acknowledge each of these positives with thanks. Oversimplified as it may seem, this is the starting point of the magic, because these thoughts enable us to tune ourselves in. In other words, we open up a channel and the thought link is direct. Starting from this point, we can then focus on what we want to draw back to us. However, this must always follow on from identification of abundance and gratitude for these things. Stating what we want without these two simple steps is not positive, so what we ask for will not materialise.

I repeat: we tune ourselves into source by acknowledging abundance and bounty all around us, it is only *after this*, that we can focus on what we need help with.

The more we do this, the more empowerment we give to ourselves. Directing our thoughts in the right ways brings life changing results.

By now I hope it is clear how damaging negative thought patterns are and that they are the biggest obstacle blocking us from our own empowerment. Negative thoughts restrain us. Positive thoughts liberate us.

Though negative thoughts come from our own thought habits, another major source in so many people I see stems from the words and behaviours of others. So, as well as managing our thoughts, we need to be constantly aware of who we are mixing with because the energy of other people feeds off and into our own constantly.

It is important to identify and deal with external sources of negativity. Sometimes, it may not be immediately obvious that someone or something is bad for us. This is why it is always vital to listen to our feelings and hear the thoughts they create inside us.

As we have explored, thoughts enable us to attract scenarios back to us that play out what we have asked for. The more we channel our thoughts, the more we attract what we want. With practise, this goes beyond the manifestation of physical things. Spiritual protection is simply an extension of what happens after we have been practising positive thinking for a while.

For many years, I didn't really understand the phenomenal power of the energy that was guiding me. I do now!!!

I have been practising this way of thinking for so long that my engagement in the loop is automatic, but the process is identical.

It is my constant link into source that enables me to do my job and tune into the energy surrounding clients who come to see me.

I put all my faith and trust in this process but it has taken a long time for me to accept this fully. I no longer need proof I just accept without question.

I never feel overburdened with worry or over faced by "issues" I cannot deal with. I know that we are never alone in our life's journey. My belief is now unshakeable

---

"However many holy words you read,
However many you speak,
what good will they do if you do not act upon them?"

Buddha

Thank you for reading

THE END

ABOUT THE AUTHOR

Lesley Metcalfe is a commissioned writer, and has written several screen and radio plays, and has been shortlisted in an international screenwriting competition.

Beyond the Five Senses is her first book.

She is currently working on a children's book and a play.

References

Bradshaw, John   *Homecoming – Reclaiming your inner child*
ISBN 13-978-0553353891

Bryne, Rhonda   *The Secret*
ISBN 13-978-1582701707

Cayce, Edgar   *Encyclopaedia of Healing*
ISBN 13-978-0446608411

Choquetta, Sonia   *Ask your Guides*
ISBN 13-978-1401907877

Cohen, Tammy   *The Day I Died*
ISBN 844542491

Cunfield, Jack   *Chicken Soup for the Soul*
ISBN 13-978-1623611118

Charles Haanel   *The Master Key* ISBN
13-978-1612930831

Hay, Louise   *Feeling Fine Affirmations*
ISBN 13-978-1401904173

     Overcoming Fears
ISBN 13-978-1401904012

	You Can Heal Your Life' ISBN 13-978-0-93-7611-01-1
Hicks, Esther & Jerry	*Ask and it is Given* ISBN 13-978-1401904593
Jeffers, Sue	*Feel the Fear and Do it Anyway* ISBN 13-978-0345487421
Modi, Shaluntala M.D.	*Remarkable Healings'* ISBN 1-57174-079-1
	• *Protection Prayer* http://www.hrpub.com.net
Mora, Eva Maria	*Quantum Angel Healing'* ISBN 13-978-1450786386
Orloff, Judith M.D.	*'Positive Energy'* ISBN 13-978-1400082162
Peale, Norman Vincent	*The Power of Positive Thinking* ISBN 0-9432-3480-4
Peck, Dr M Scott M.D.	*The Road Less Traveled* ISBN 13-978-0743243155
Redfield, James	*Celestine Prophecy* ISBN 13-978-0446671002

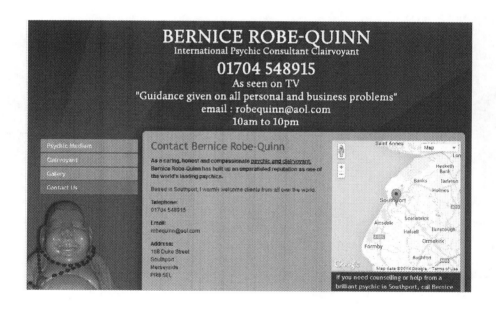